The Purity Principle

The Purity Principle

FINDING AUTHENTICITY
IN THE AGE OF DECEPTION

Eighteen Teachings on Transcendence

SWAMI B. B. BODHAYAN

MANDALA
San Rafael • Los Ángeles • London

MANDALA
PUBLISHING

PO Box 3088
San Rafael, CA 94912
www.mandalaearth.com
info@mandala.org

Find us on Facebook: www.facebook.com/mandalaearth
Follow us on Twitter: @mandalaearth

Published by Mandala Publishing, San Rafael, California, in 2020.

Library of Congress Cataloging-in-Publication Data available.

ISBN: 978-1-64722-160-7

Readers interested in the subject matter should visit the Gopinath Gaudiya Math website at www.gopinathgaudiyamath.com or write to:

Ishodyan, Sri Mayapur
District Nadia, West Bengal
India, 741313

Manufactured in India

vande 'haṁ śrī-guroḥ śrī-yuta-pada-kamalaṁ śrī-gurūn vaiṣṇavāṁś ca
śrī-rūpaṁ sāgrajātaṁ saha-gaṇa-raghunāthānvitaṁ taṁ sa-jīvam
sādvaitaṁ sāvadhūtaṁ parijana-sahitaṁ kṛṣṇa-caitanya-devaṁ
śrī-rādhā-kṛṣṇa-pādān saha-gaṇa-lalitā-śrī-viśākhānvitāṁś ca

I offer my most respectful obeisances unto the lotus feet of my divine preceptor and my instructing gurus. I offer my most respectful obeisances unto all the Vaiṣṇavas and unto the Six Gosvāmīs, including Śrīla Rūpa Gosvāmī, Śrīla Sanātana Gosvāmī, Raghunātha Dāsa Gosvāmī, Jīva Gosvāmī, and their associates. I offer my respectful obeisances unto Śrī Advaita Ācārya Prabhu, Śrī Nityānanda Prabhu, Śrī Caitanya Mahāprabhu, and all His devotees, headed by Śrīvāsa Ṭhākura. I then offer my respectful obeisances unto the lotus feet of Lord Kṛṣṇa, Śrīmatī Rādhārāṇī, and all the *gopīs*, headed by Lalitā and Viśākhā.

Śrīla Bhakti Pramode Purī Gosvāmī Ṭhākura
Founder Ācārya, Śrī Gopīnātha Gauḍīya Maṭha

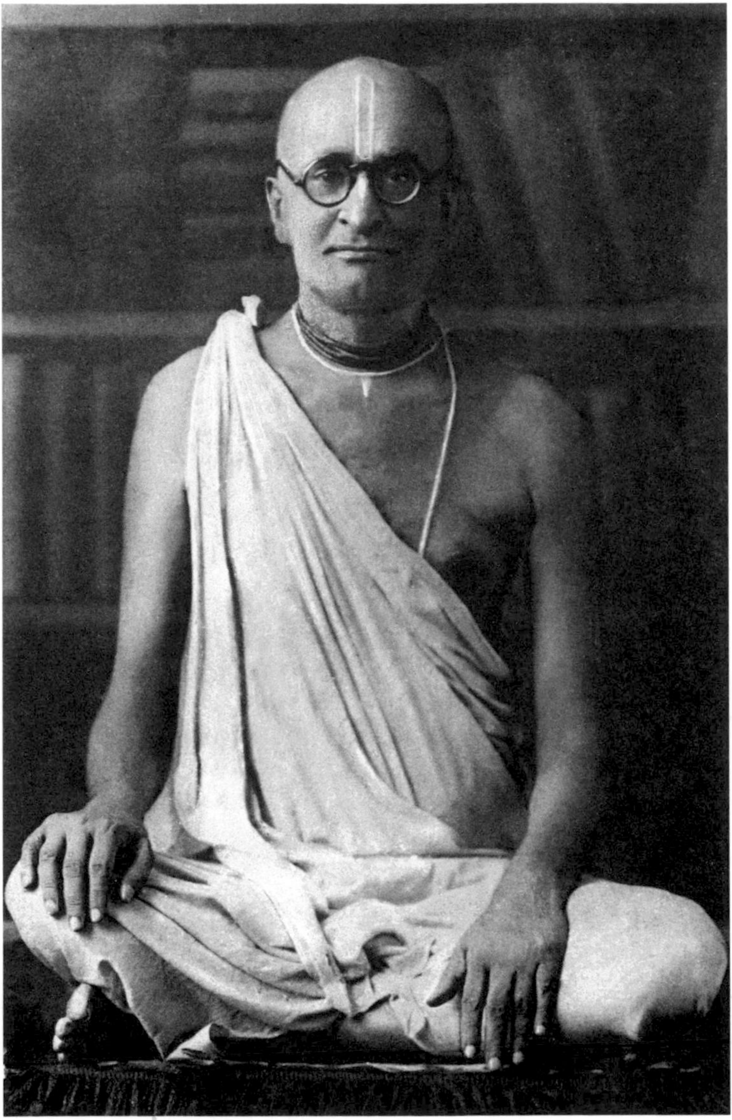

Śrīla Bhaktisiddhānta Sarasvatī Ṭhākura Prabhupāda

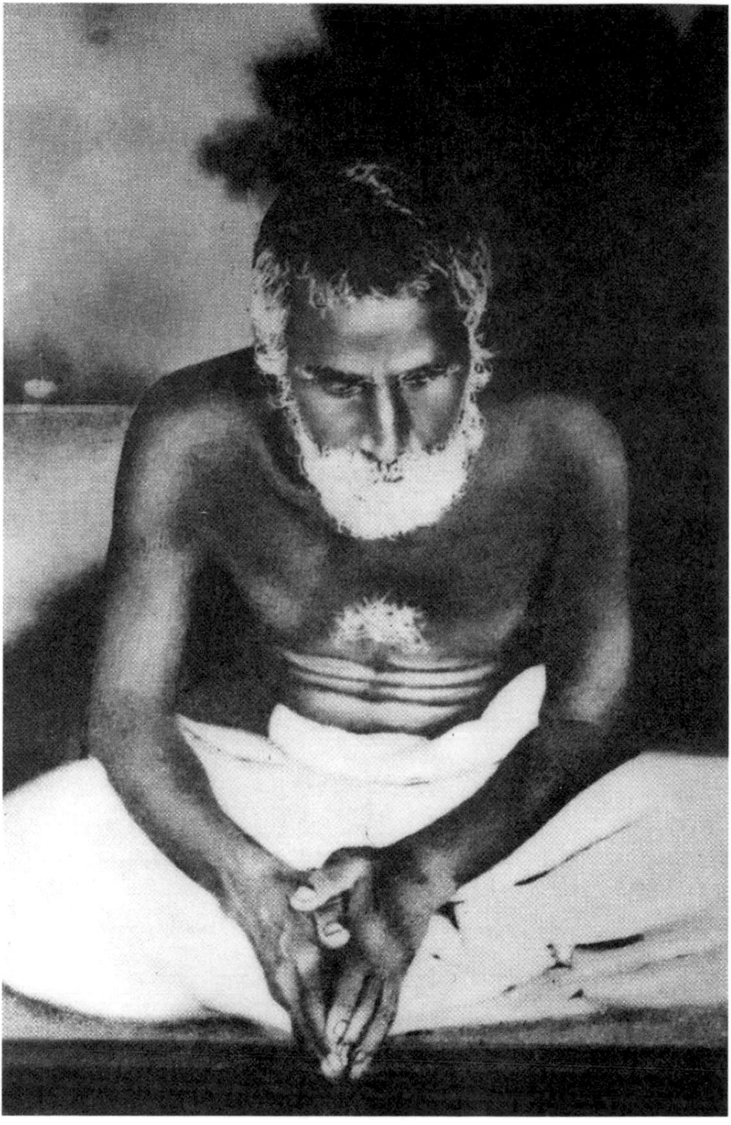

Śrīla Gaurakiśora dāsa Bābājī Mahārāja

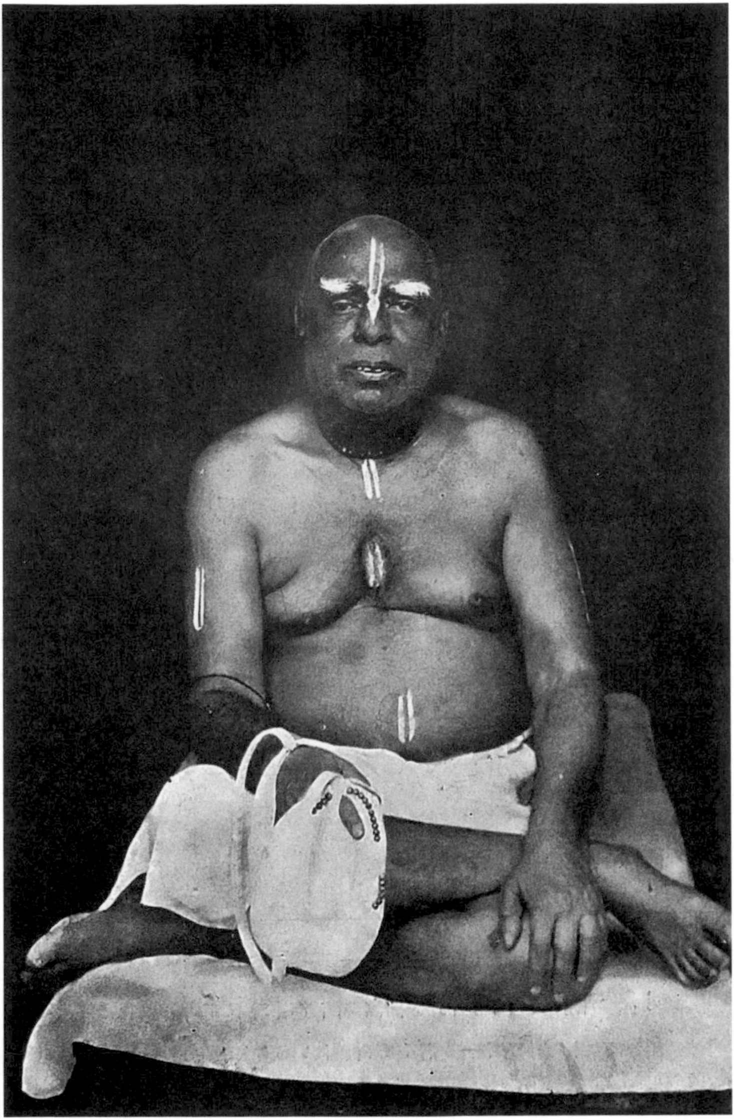

Śrīla Saccidānanda Bhaktivinoda Ṭhākura

Contents

Introduction

Swami B. B. Bodhayan

These days in society, qualities like spirituality, religiousness, simplicity, generosity, and so on, are widely talked about and appreciated, but those who have developed affinities for these qualities may wonder about their source along with their connection to our origins. Wise and thoughtful persons may consider that these qualities may be attributed to the source of our existence, and that's what makes them so attractive. If we look deeper and examine these qualities, we will easily come to the conclusion: God is their source.

Someone once asked a tree, "Who are you?" The tree responded, "I am known by my fruits" (*phalena pariciyate*). God is the source-tree of all living beings; hence His qualities, His fruits, by definition, are reflected in all beings, and through those fruits the tree is revealed. God, being the Supreme Creator, has all qualities in full. He is also eternally blissful, peaceful, and full of love.

Although we are His parts and parcels,

however, these qualities are not found in us. Why? This is because we are suffering the consequences of our previous misdeeds, which have covered us with myriad unwanted material desires that impede our ability to manifest our spiritual qualities. These qualities are actually present in all of us but in a dormant state, and as soon as we become purified from the contamination of material desires through spiritual practice, the qualities will automatically be revealed from within. Each age recommends a specific spiritual practice. In this age, the age of quarrel and hypocrisy, the Age of Kali, the prescribed practice is to chant the holy names of God.

The living entities are not their temporary material bodies; they are eternal souls who have emanated from God (the Supersoul). At the time of death, the soul, being eternal, gives up whatever temporary body it is inhabiting and takes another birth. This is part of a perpetual cycle of birth and death known as *samsara*. Due to the fruits of its actions (*karma-phala*), the soul acquires a particular type of new body after each death, and this continues life after life. Lord Brahma is the first living being in the material creation and the predominating deity of the mode of passion, and is responsible for creating the various types of bodies for the living beings. Through meditation, he came to the realization that Lord Krishna is the Supreme Being (God) and the source of all souls. Lord Brahma expresses this point in the *Brahma-samhita,* which provides scriptural evidence that Lord Krishna is the origin of all. Sri Krishna Himself declares this in the *Bhagavad Gita*: *mamaivamsho jiva loke jiva bhuta sanatana* – "All living entities are My eternal separated parts and parcels."

Although science tries to make sense of the world around us, it is not free from controversies, debates, and uncertainties. Scientific theories and facts are based on tangible evidence, but over time and through advancements in technology, theories change. We can define changing theories as impermanent ideas, and conclude that impermanent ideas are unreliable; they cannot be considered facts, or truth. For example, in their search for truth, scientists have come up with the theory of evolution – still a hotly debated topic both in religious and scientific circles. Note the word *theory* here. Although scientists claim to have evidence proving evolution by natural selection, that evidence is not conclusive and the subject matter remains, therefore, theoretical. It cannot be taken as fact. Rather, it is a hypothesis, or supposition. *Hypothesis* is another way to say *theory*. There are subject areas in the theory of evolution, such as transmutation of species, that have remained controversial even among biologists and scientists in other fields.

It is worth noting that science has a muddy idea on the origin of life. Some theories state that life began as a single-cell microorganism billions of years ago, that humans evolved from primates and therefore share a common ancestor with primates. When analyzed deeply, however, we see that Darwin's theory of evolution contains a number of flaws. His idea of evolution through natural selection doesn't answer all questions on how certain living organisms came into being, and there is nothing substantial for some of his propositions, since they are only theoretical ideas.

In our spiritual tradition we do not believe that we evolved from either microorganisms or primates, nor do we believe that we share common ancestors with either of these. Rather, we are the direct descendants of Manu, the progenitor of humankind. Manu was the son of Brahma, as scripture states. The knowledge we've received from the scriptures is unchanged, unmodified, and completely perfect because it comes down from the Perfect Person, God, Sri Krishna. This knowledge is eternal and is accepted as the ultimate truth, without debate.

Spiritual knowledge, as it is presented in the Vedic literature, has existed since time immemorial. Although the Vedas are known to have been recorded some five thousand years ago, the knowledge they contain and the practice of it, called Vaishnavism, have always existed. Sri Krishna spoke the *Bhagavad Gita* around the same time the Vedic scriptures were written down. The *Bhagavad Gita* is part of the *Mahabharata*. Although Sri Krishna spoke the *Bhagavad Gita* in the previous age, He never taught it widely. Therefore, He appeared again, in the form of Lord Chaitanya in Kali-yuga, to teach how to practice this magnanimous spirituality known as Vaishnavism.

Lord Chaitanya made his appearance in Mayapur, Nadia, West Bengal, in 1486 during the twilight hours of a lunar eclipse on the full-moon day of the Bengali month Phalguna (February–March). His mission was to disseminate Vaishnavism and to establish the practice for this age, chanting the holy names of God. In this connection I would like to describe how ancient this knowledge is by describing the source of creation delineated in the Vedas.

Sri Krishna, being the original Personality of Godhead, is the source of all incarnations, and from Him, many other divine forms are manifest. At first, He expands into four such forms: Vasudeva, Sankarshana, Pradyumna, and Aniruddha. In order to serve and assist Sri Krishna with the material creation, Sankarshana expands further into five forms: Karanodakashayi Vishnu, Garbhodakashayi Vishnu, Kshirodakashayi Vishnu, Maha-Sankarshana, and Ananta-Shesha. Although Sankarshana is the origin of these five forms, the first of them will manifest another and another form, and so on. From Karanodakashayi Vishnu comes Garbhodakashayi Vishnu. A divine lotus grows from the navel of Garbhodakashayi Vishnu containing the fourteen planetary systems. As described earlier, Lord Brahma is the first created being in this universe, and he spontaneously appears atop that lotus according to the Lord's will. Trying to understand his own purpose and existence, Brahma practiced penance, and divine spiritual knowledge was revealed in his heart by Sri Krishna. On receiving this knowledge, Brahma practiced Vaishnavism and then commenced the creation of living forms in order to please Sri Krishna.

From the description of creation, we can understand that Vaishnavism is a very ancient practice, having existed since the first living being. Through his practice Brahma realized the purpose of his existence and his position in relation to God. Vaishnavism addresses consciousness of the soul and the loving connection with God through service. It is nothing like mundane religiosity, which deals only with the selfish satisfaction of body, mind, and intelligence. This focus on the soul's relationship with God is why the practice of Vaishnavism can be described as magnanimous spirituality.

In the present society there is much conflict between religions. Everyone demands that their religion is superior to others. Such sectarian and judgmental mentalities are the cause of the world's chaos. If we read the history of the different religions it will be clear that over the ages people have been forced to follow one path or another; otherwise, they would be punished, even killed, by the hierarchies within those religions.

However, the magnanimous spiritual practice of Vaishnavism is of a completely different nature. It focuses not on mundane externalities but on the soul, which is the actual identity of each living entity. If we observe the soul through the evidence of scripture we can see that based on its actions and their consequences, souls take birth in various physical forms, such as those of aquatics, plants and other nonmoving living entities, reptiles, worms, birds, nonhuman mammals, and humans. We can also observe that apart from the human form, living entities in all other forms act only on instinct. For example, cows are herbivorous and eat only plant-based foods. Even a starving cow presented with meat will not eat it even to save its life, because instinctively it knows only to eat plants (except onions and garlic). I mention that cows don't eat onions and garlic or meat even for survival because according to Vaishnavism, the flesh of the cow is connected to the creation of onions and garlic. Some cows have a natural instinct not to eat those plants. Humans have a different nature and do not function solely on instinct. Instead, God has given them both intelligence and free will. Humans adopt their nature, culture, food habits, and so on, through association. Therefore, we see that all humans are physiologically the same but different in terms of their culture, what they eat, what they believe in, and the languages they speak.

Humans have been given the best intelligence among all living beings, yet due to the influence of the current age, despite being equipped with superior intelligence we quarrel and act hypocritically. We make various attempts to establish an optimal way to achieve peace and happiness, but then aggressively force our ideas on others and blatantly commit violence against those who don't agree with us – all in the name of religion.

The path of magnanimous spirituality is of a different nature. It has no connection at all with the material world. The only connection it has is with the soul and God. This is what makes it the most magnanimous path. Focused solely on spirit, magnanimous spirituality is free of sectarianism and doesn't judge other paths or force itself on others. Instead, it works with an individual's desire to understand the self.

On achieving a human body, souls become eligible to practice spirituality and to cure the disease of material attachment to the body and everything in relation to the body. Spiritual practice includes gradually realizing that we are not the body we're inhabiting, but spirit soul. Other than souls in a human form, no other living entity can practice spirituality. Spiritual practice allows us to fix the mind on God and be delivered by Him from the cycle of birth and death. Since time immemorial, the soul has been afflicted by the disease of attachment to material objects, and the only vehicle available to fix the soul's defects is the human form of life.

What exactly is the methodology for fixing this defect? It is chanting the holy names of God, as taught by Lord Chaitanya.

According to *Srimad-Bhagavatam* and other ancient scriptures, we know that Krishna is the Supreme Personality of Godhead. When Krishna descends to earth He reveals His various pastimes in locations like Dvaraka, Mathura, Vrindavan, and other places. His sweetest pastimes, known as the *madhurya-lila,* were performed in Vrindavan – pastimes He performed to attract the hearts of all living entities. When that same sweet Vrindavan Krishna later appears as Lord Chaitanya, He spreads magnanimous spirituality, called in Sanskrit His *audarya-lila,* and thereby conquers the wicked ways of humankind by establishing a religion of sweetness and magnanimity. In that regard, Lord Chaitanya taught us the importance of developing qualities like humility, tolerance, being free from the tendency to worship matter in one form or another, detachment from interest in material gain, name, and fame, and respect for others. Developing such qualities helps us eradicate our wicked tendencies and enables us to practice the spiritual path with purity. These qualities will manifest in the heart through pure chanting, and they are the prime basis of Vaishnavism. In essence, these Vaishnava qualities aim at purifying our hearts so that we can chant purely and focus on the Lord's qualities rather than on fulfilling materialistic desires.

Śrīla Bhakti Bibudha Bodhāyan Mahārāja
President Ācārya, Śrī Gopīnātha Gauḍīya Maṭha

A Note About This Book

My inspiration for this book came from a poem written by my grand spiritual master, His Divine Grace Srila Bhaktisiddhanta Saraswati Thakur Prabhupada. Using this poem *Vaishnava Ke?*, which was originally written in Bengali, I will attempt to explore the qualities of a Vaishnava and comment on elements that may pose as obstacles on the spiritual path. I will also touch on other topics in order to bring more clarity to the idea of magnanimous spirituality. Before delving into the poem, however, I would first like to present the three basic levels of Vaishnavas as Lord Chaitanya presented them:

1. Uttama (topmost) Vaishnavas: They see the Lord's presence in all living beings and perceive only good in others regardless of that being's character. People are attracted to them because of their humility, tolerance, and other pure Vaishnava qualities, and

therefore are inspired to chant the Lord's holy names.

2. *Madhyama* (intermediate) Vaishnavas: They have the ability to discriminate between favorable and unfavorable association and qualities within the different species of life. They understand the importance of associating with Vaishnavas for their spiritual progress, and they constantly chant the Lord's holy names with pure intention.
3. *Kanistha* (neophyte) Vaishnavas: They repose their faith in the guru and the Deity but not in other Vaishnavas. They periodically chant the Lord's names with purity. We should understand that the *kanistha* mentality creates chaos in a community of Vaishnavas.

The qualities of the Vaishnavas described above are fruits of their qualitative connection with the Supreme Lord and His devotees. They are manifest from the heart and cannot be imitated—they are the result of purity on the path of bhakti. In this book, the principle of purity is elaborated upon in order to help distinguish the sincere and authentic character of the Vaishnava and to help us avoid deviation and imitation in its many forms. These pure and authentic qualities have been characterized as *magnanimous spirituality,* as they are spilling over from the unlimited reservoir of bhakti that is transmitted by the Lord and His pure devotees in a causeless and benevolent manner. We simply need to step into that eternal grace of the Vaishnavas, and try and catch the waves of their mercy. I pray that you will find hope and inspiration in the pages of *The Purity Principle.*

Vaishnava Ke?

(What Kind of Devotee Are You?)

---

bhupada Bhaktisiddhanta
Saraswati Thakur

TRANSLATION AND COMMENTARY BY
Swami B. B. Bodhayan

Text 1

duṣṭa mana! tumi kiśera vaiṣṇava?
pratiṣṭhāra tare, nirjanera ghare,
tava 'harināma' kevala 'kaitava'
jaḍera pratiṣṭhā, śūkarera viṣṭhā,
jana nā ki tāhā 'māyāra vaibhava'

Word-for-word

duṣṭa – wicked; *mana* – mind; *tumi* – you; *kiśera* – what type; *vaiṣṇava* – practitioner of magnanimous spirituality; *pratiṣṭhā* – material name and fame; *tare* – for; *nirjanera ghare* – in a lonely room; *tava* – your; *harināma* – chanting of the holy names; *kevala* – only; *kaitava* – hypocritical; *jaḍera pratiṣṭhā* – desire for material name and fame; *śūkarera viṣṭhā* – stool of a hog; *jana nā ki* – don't you know; *tāhā* – it is; *māyāra vaibhava* – opulence of illusion.

Translation

O wicked mind! How can you say that you are practicing the path of magnanimous spirituality?

You are sitting alone in a room and chanting the holy names, but that is just a show of hypocrisy. Don't you know that the desire to gain material name and fame is just like the stool of a hog, which is the dirtiest quality in the material world? Don't you know that it is the opulence of illusion?

Commentary

Practicing magnanimous spirituality cleanses all dirt from the mind, intelligence, consciousness, and heart. Sometimes people make a show of being elevated by dint of renunciation, sitting in a lonely place and chanting while internally desiring material name, fame, and distinction. Most people believe in such pretenders, who outwardly exhibit wonderful qualities and appear attractive. But when we closely examine these so-called spiritual practitioners we see that their hearts are full of dirt, full of selfish motivations. People who become attracted to pretenders eventually lose their faith in the path of magnanimous spirituality. Those who want to practice the genuine path of magnanimous spirituality serve under the guidance of currently living teachers and previous teachers in the line. Isolating ourselves and chanting without the guidance of such teachers in a bona fide line of disciplic succession only increases our material attachments. That chanting does not, then, produce spiritual fruits. But the goal of spiritual practice is to free ourselves from material attachment and to increase our spiritual attachment.

His Divine Grace Srila Bhaktisiddhanta Saraswati Thakur Prabhupada wanted to spread the loving mission of Chaitanya Mahaprabhu according to the instructions of his previous teachers. It takes preparation to embark on such a mission, and this is usually done through intense spiritual practice and austerities. Through his own example Srila Prabhupada taught the world how to attract the mercy and blessings of both his contemporary and his previous teachers. He did this by fulfilling his vow to chant one billion names of the Lord before embarking on his preaching mission. To chant one billion names means chanting 192 rounds of the Hare Krishna *maha-mantra* every day for nine or ten years. Within one year of each other, between 1914 and 1915, Srila Prabhupada's teachers, Srila Bhaktivinode Thakur and Srila Gour Kishore Das

Babaji Maharaj, both disappeared from the material world. Srila Prabhupada felt he had lost his shelter. He didn't know how he could deliver others when his own two sources of shelter were gone. He also thought that his two teachers were shelter for others, and now that they had disappeared, he had no one to whom he could bring people for deliverance. Therefore he decided he would sit in Vrindavan for the rest of his life and chant.

Then one day, while he was chanting early in the morning, Srila Prabhupada had a divine vision in which he saw all of his previous teachers, including Bhaktivinode Thakur, Gour Kishore Das Babaji Maharaj, the Six Goswamis, and the Panca-tattva. They instructed Srila Prabhupada not to simply chant for the rest of his life. They conveyed to him instead that he was to spread the message of divine love throughout the world. At that time, Srila Prabhupada expressed a concern: "If I am to spread the loving message of the Lord, I need manpower." His teachers replied as one: "We will send you manpower. Don't worry."

And Srila Prabhupada was sent many associates to assist him in spreading the mission of Lord Chaitanya. Therefore, we consider all of Srila Prabhupada's disciples to be spiritual descendants of Lord Chaitanya. Some of Srila Prabhupada's associates were Bhakti Vilas Tirtha Goswami Thakur (previously known as Kunja Babu), Bhakti Prajnan Keshav Goswami Thakur (previously known as Vinod Da), Bhakti Pramode Puri Goswami Thakur, Bhakti Dayita Madhav Goswami Thakur, Bhakti Rakshak Sridhar Goswami Thakur, Bhaktivedanta Swami Goswami Thakur, Bhakti Gaurav Vaikhanas Goswami Thakur, Bhakti Hrday Bon Goswami Thakur, Bhakti Kusum Sraman Goswami Thakur, Bhakti Kumud Sant Goswami Thakur, Bhakti Vaibhav Puri Goswami Thakur, Bhakti Saranga Goswami Thakur, Bhakti Pradip Tirtha Goswami Thakur, and Bhakti Keval Audulomi Thakur. Each of them was an exemplary person, showing us how to practice the path of magnanimous spirituality under the guidance of the previous teachers.

Before propagating the message of the *Bhagavat*, our purpose is to first develop Vaishnava qualities by chanting the holy names. Instead of serving others, if we ourselves expect to be served because we have made a show of austerity and renunciation, this is hypocrisy. Genuine renunciation attracts the attention of the Supreme Lord, but deceptive renunciation attracts only the attention of ignorant people. It will never bring divine love, the supreme goal of life, to fruition. Deceptive renunciation – renunciation practiced only to gain material name and fame – is only pretense. Once we become attached to name and fame it's very difficult to remove that desire from the heart and consciousness. Instead, such attachment drags us deeper into the dark, dry well of material existence. This verse compares this attachment to the stool of a hog. Hogs eat all types of dirt, so one can imagine what kind of stool they produce. When we run after material name and fame and win the opulence they generate, we may think ourselves fortunate, but such achievements only drag us deeper into material existence. It's not the goal of human life to be dragged into a deep, dark, dry well of material existence. Rather, the goal is to climb out of the well and ascend to the divine realm of service to the Divine Couple in a life of eternal and blissful *seva*.

To become qualified to serve the Divine Couple in this age of quarrel and hypocrisy we have to chant the holy name and simultaneously serve under the guidance of a guru and the previous teachers. I'm sure if one practices spirituality under the guidance of the previous teachers, serving

Vaishnavas as prescribed by Lord Chaitanya, one will definitely gain the ability to fix the mind, intelligence, consciousness, and heart on chanting. *Prabhu kahe vaiṣṇava sevana āra nāma saṅkīrtana / ei dui kara pābe kṛṣṇera caraṇa.* Here the word *vaiṣṇava* indicates *guru* and the previous teachers. By serving the guru and Vaishnavas, we receive their blessings and so can chant the Lord's names with purity. These two things – Vaishnava blessings and pure chanting – will allow us to enter into the Supreme Lord's eternal abode and render service to Him, which is the eternal function and identity of all living entities.

Text 2

kanaka-kāminī divasa-yāminī
bhāviyā ki kāja, anitya se saba
tomāra kanaka, bhogera janaka,
kanakera dvāre sevaha 'mādhava'

Word-for-word

kanaka – material wealth; *kāminī* – women or sensual desires; *divasa* – day; *yāminī* – night; *bhāviyā* – thinking; *ki* – what; *kāja* – utility; *anitya* – temporary; *se saba* – all that; *tomāra* – your; *kanaka* – material wealth; *bhogera janaka* – father of enjoyment; *kanaker dvāre* – through material wealth; *sevaha* – serve; *mādhava* – the Supreme Lord (Krishna).

Translation

What is the point of thinking about material wealth, women, and sensual desires all day and night? They are all temporary. Your material wealth is the source of your desire for material sense enjoyment. It is better for you to serve the Supreme Lord, Madhava, with your material wealth.

Commentary

Nowadays, people are unable to realize the consequences of engaging with the material energy. The material energy makes us think what is untrue to be true. The material energy's influence is increasing day by day and, because they are influenced by it most people choose to use their wealth to fulfill their sense desires. Like donkeys, they work busily day and night. They live like hyenas. It may make you uneasy to hear me say this, but hyenas are known to be very territorial animals. During the day, for their survival they tend to roam a large amount of land, but at night they occupy only as much ground as their bodies can sleep on. Similarly, in order to fulfill their desires for sense gratification, people build big, beautiful residences, taking up much space for their living arrangements, but when it comes to sleeping, they are just like hyenas, except instead of sleeping on the ground they sleep on a bed that usually only occupies about 1.5–2 meters. What's the use, then, of their vast living arrangements?

It's now normal for people to work hard day and night in order to earn the money to construct these palatial residences, built for the sole purpose of maximizing their sense gratification. This is the way of modern materialistic civilization. People then arrange parties in these homes, serving wine and performing various other mode-of-ignorance activities harmful to the soul. They also destroy the innocence of their impressionable children. Due to their infatuation with material enjoyment and in order to support their unlimited desires, these materialists constantly develop and modify technology. They want to make others mad after their products. But we can see that people aren't happy despite the most advanced technological products. Rather, they are becoming more and more distressed.

All the distress we experience in our human lives is because we aren't engaging our abilities in thinking about the Lord's satisfaction and pleasure, which is supposed to be the main purpose of our existence. If we carefully analyze the material creation, we'll understand that it has been created by the Lord and that He is its owner. By the influence of the material energy, we always think that whatever we occupy belongs to us and is meant for our sense gratification.

Let me give an example. Someone owns a beautiful house in Paris, one of the most artistic cities in the world. Now, if we ask the owner of that house, "Who owns this house?" the owner will typically say, "It's my house." But is it really his house? Even though the owner may have all the documents that prove ownership, if we look carefully, we'll see that the house is in Paris. Where is Paris? It's in France. Where is France? In Europe. Where is Europe? It's on Earth. Who owns the Earth? Since we have already established that the Lord is the creator, then naturally, He is the owner of the Earth. Therefore, in all respects the house really belongs to the Lord. When the so-called deeded owner finally leaves his body at death, the house remains with everything else the deeded owner possessed. Everything in the material world is temporary, but we, the spirit soul, are an eternal tiny existential form of the Lord, created by the Lord. The conclusion is that the Lord is the ultimate owner and creator of everything.

Somehow, due to our ignorance, we think ourselves the owners of everything we see, and because of this misconception we engage ourselves in enjoying the Lord's creation without respecting His ownership of it. The result of doing anything without honoring the Lord is that we inevitably accrue karma. This karmic activity binds us to the material world. If we think about the goal of our actions – the results we are after when performing them – we'll find that we're looking for an eternal outcome. Aiming for eternal happiness is natural to us because our origin is eternal and happy. But our happiness is constantly being interrupted by the material energy. This is due to our entanglement in karma caused by our attempts to enjoy the Lord's property.

Running after material opulence in order to achieve that happiness is fruitless because matter is not eternal; its temporality can lead only to dissatisfaction. In reality, chasing after wealth is the root cause of why we are driven to engage with the material energy. What is the outcome? We are snared by the material, illusory energy. However, if we want to apply our talents to making our lives real – free from material illusion – then we should use our material wealth for the service of the Supreme Lord Madhava (Krishna). Lord Madhava, is complete and self-satisfied. He does not want to take anything from us, nor does he need anything from us; He is, after all, the owner of the entire material universe. Yet if somehow we engage whatever wealth we have in His service, we can become free from karmic entanglement.

In this human form, instead of instinct as our only driving force, we also have great talent, intelligence, and free will. One who pursues eternality should be considered to be a talented person, because pursuing eternality means engaging in spiritual practice, and spiritual practice means to constantly fix one's consciousness, mind, heart, intelligence, and activities on the Supreme Lord. To be so fixed in consciousness is not an ordinary act; that's why I call it a talent.

We understand from this second of His Divine Grace Bhaktisiddhanta Saraswati Thakur Prabhupada's verses that Prabhupada is instructing us to fix our minds on serving Madhava at every step. We will not lose anything; rather, we shall gain the opportunity to enter the eternal blissful abode of the Supreme Lord. This is the main goal of all living beings – to become eternally blissful.

Text 3

kāminīra kāma, nahe tava dhāma
tāhara mālika – kevala 'yādava'
pratiṣṭhāśā-taru, jaḍa-māyā-maru,
nā pela 'rāvaṇa' yujhiyā 'rāghava'

Word-for-word

kāminīra kāma – lust for a woman; *nahe* – is not; *tava* – your; *dhāma* – final destination; *tāhara mālika* – the owner of enjoyment; *kevala* – only; *yādava* – the Supreme Lord, Yadava, or Vasudeva Krishna; *pratiṣṭh*āśā – desire for material name and fame; *taru* – tree; *jaḍā* – material; *māyā* – illusion; *maru* – desert; *nā* – did not; *pela* – get; *rāvaṇa* – a demon who ruled Lanka during Lord Ramachandra's time; *yujhiyā* – fighting; *rāghava* – Lord Ramachandra.

Translation

According to the Vedic explanation, there are five objects of sense enjoyment, namely form (*rupa*), taste (*rasa*), sound (*shabda*), fragrance (*gandha*), and touch (*sparsha*). The combination of these five objects of sense enjoyment is called "woman" (*kamini*). Enjoying the opposite sex [a man trying to enjoy a woman or a woman a man] in order to fulfill one's sense desires is not our ultimate purpose. Actually, the ultimate enjoyer is the Supreme Lord, Vasudeva.

Commentary

Having read the above, readers may believe that the verse means it's not proper to marry, because relations with the opposite sex are improper. But the goal of marriage and conceiving children is to serve the Lord. Every aspect of married life should be aimed at serving the Lord. If this ideal is maintained, then there is no question of marriage being about mundane sense enjoyment; rather, it is considered service to the Lord and a means by which the Supreme Lord's service will be continued into the future. Married couples quickly realize that raising a child with proper consciousness is a great challenge in today's society. All aspects of today's society teach children to fix their minds solely on material gain. However, spiritually sincere human beings balance material duties with spiritual responsibilities. That we need to find this balance is something that must be imbibed in childhood.

They say, "A first impression is a lasting impression." Children are very impressionable, and from a young age they pay attention and learn by observing the behavior of their parents and the others around them. Sincere parents have the responsibility to teach their children spiritual practice along with how to perform their material duties for the sake of the Lord's services. In most circumstances, children who grow up with a spiritual culture don't fix their minds solely on material gain. In this manner, then, a man and a woman come together in marriage in order to serve the Lord. The goal of their married life is not to satisfy their senses but to create a way to continue the Lord's services after their demise. This type of marriage is part of devotional practice.

When people suffer from scorching heat they seek shelter in the shade of a tree. But in the desert, although there are occasional trees, there is absolutely no shade. The only "trees" growing in a desert are thorny cacti. Instead of providing relief-giving shade, as one would expect from a tree, one expects only pain from the cacti's sharp thorns. This pain is the consequence of material attachment. Yet we constantly try to find enjoyment by attempting to fulfill our material desires, thinking that mundane pleasure will give us cool relief and happiness in the hot desert of material existence. Instead, we feel distress and pain in the desert of illusory material existence, with no relief at all.

Material name, fame, and distinction is a desert mirage. Thirsty people run behind mirages in order to quench their thirst. We all know that a mirage is the reflection of the sun on sand, but mirages can be seen from a distance, and people afflicted by thirst mistake them for water and feverishly run toward them. But no matter how far they run, the "water" remains always out of reach. People who desire material name, fame, and distinction always think about how to achieve these goals, but such goals also remain out of reach because, like the people in the desert, these materialists are chasing a mirage. Name and fame are impermanent and don't bring us eternal happiness. People die while trying to fulfill their illusory desires.

In the *Ramayana* we see how the demon Ravana fought against the Supreme Lord, Raghava, Lord Ramachandra. Ravana, who was the personification of the demonic nature, had a strong desire to use his abilities to defeat Lord Rama. Gradually Ravana lost all his affectionate sons along with many of his other male relatives and his friends. He also lost his power and position. Then he died. Our material desires are like Ravana's unquenchable thirst to fulfill his material ambitions. All of us are uselessly running behind our material ambitions and wasting our valuable human lives for nothing. We gradually accumulate the consequences of our bad karma, which brings us repeatedly back to the cycle of birth and death. We are then unable to be delivered from that material cycle and gain entrance to the eternally blissful spiritual abode.

In this verse, His Divine Grace Srila Bhaktisiddhanta Saraswati Thakur Prabhupada reminds us of the ultimate value of our human body and how to strategically navigate through various negative material influences. By following this process, we can eventually fix our minds on the Supreme Lord, be delivered from the material cycle, and gain entrance into the eternally blissful spiritual abode. Rather than fulfilling our desires for sense enjoyment and fighting with Raghava, better to dedicate all of our life's activities to His service.

Text 4

vaiṣṇavī pratiṣṭhā, tāte kara niṣṭhā,
tāhā nā bhajile labhibe raurava
harijana-dveṣa, pratiṣṭhāśā-kleśa,
kara kena tabe tāhāra gaurava

Word-for-word

vaiṣṇavī pratiṣṭhā – being established in the quality of magnanimous spirituality (pure Vaishnava qualities); *tāte* – in that; *kara* – keep; *niṣṭhā* – firm faith; *tāhā* – that; *nā bhajile* – if one does not practice; *labhibe* – will attain; *raurava* – hell; *harijana* – pure devotees of Hari; *dveṣa* – hate; *pratiṣṭhāśā-kleśa* – futile endeavor for material name and fame; *kara* – do; *kena* – why; *tabe* – in that case; *tāhāra gaurava* – glorify that.

Translation

Keep sound faith in pure Vaishnava qualities. If you do not engage in spiritual practice in order to develop these qualities, then the influences of the material world will pull you to hell. Even though you know you will attain a hellish condition, why do you continue glorifying the practice of hating pure devotees of Hari and endeavoring for material name and fame?

Commentary

According to the philosophy of magnanimous spirituality, the desire for material name and fame is as unclean as the stool of a hog. In this verse, *vaishnava pratistha* means that we should establish the twenty-six Vaishnava qualities in our consciousness. The twenty-six qualities are: *kripalu* – mercifulness; *akrita-droha* – freedom from enmity; *satya-sara* – accepting the essential truth; *sama* – being equal in all circumstances; *nidosha* – having no faults and not seeing the faults in others; *vadanya* – magnanimity; *mridu* – being soft by nature; *shuchi* – internal and external cleanliness; *akinchana* – having no material attachments; *sarvopakaraka* – being helpful to everyone; *shanta* – peacefulness; *krishnaika-sharana* – considering Krishna one's one and only shelter; *akama* – being free from lusty desires; *nirniha* – freedom from the competitive spirit; *sthira* – fixedness; *vijita-shad-guna* – having attained the six qualities of enthusiasm, determination, patience, engaging in activities to progress on the path of devotion, giving up bad association, and following in the footsteps of the pure devotees; *mita-bhuk* – eating only as much *prasadam* as required; *apramatta* – attentiveness; *manada* – respect toward all; *amani* – not expecting material worship, gain, name, or fame; *gambhira* – gravity; *karuna* – compassion; *maitra* – friendliness; *kavi* – being poetic; *daksha* – skillfulness, expertise; *mauni* – speaking only as much as is required and remaining silent at other times.

When we're able to practice each of these qualities with sound faith, we will be able to attain the Lord's abode; if we don't practice them, we will simply go to hell. Among the twenty-six qualities, considering Krishna one's only shelter (*krishnaika-sharana*) is key to all the others. The goal of Lord Chaitanya's teachings is to inspire us to chant the Hare Krishna *maha-mantra*. Taking shelter in the holy name is *krishnaika-sharana*. The Hare Krishna *maha-mantra* gradually cleanses all the dirt from our hearts and allows us to attain divine love, *prema*. If we attain divine love, we'll drown in an ocean of blissful service to Sri Sri Radha-Govinda.

Nowadays, influenced by the material nature and in the name of chanting the Hare Krishna *maha-mantra* and practicing Vaishnava principles, people criticize pure devotees in an attempt to establish that they are superior to devotees. Furthermore, they endeavor greatly to increase their material name, gain, and worship. Although such people know that the consequence of hating pure devotees is that they will fall into a hellish condition, they nevertheless proudly engage in such activities for the sake of material name and fame. They are running rapidly toward hell, just as moths fly into a fire, enchanted by its golden glare.

Here in this verse, His Divine Grace Srila Prabhupada Bhaktisiddhanta Saraswati Thakur is instructing us to keep ourselves aloof from material name, fame, distinction, and so on. He especially instructs us not to criticize the Lord's pure devotees because such criticism is the most dangerous offense we can commit. Offenses to Vaishnavas are the greatest obstacle we face in attaining our ultimate destination, the eternally blissful abode of the Divine Couple, Sri Sri Radha-Krishna, Goloka Vrindavan.

Text 5

vaiṣṇavera pāche, pratiṣṭhā āche,
tā'ta, kabhu nahe 'anitya-vaibhava'
se hari-sambandha, śūnya-māyāgandha,
tāhā kabhu naya 'jaḍera kaitava'

Word-for-word

vaiṣṇavera pāche – behind the pure devotee Vaishnavas; *pratiṣṭhā* – name and fame; *āche* – have; *tā'ta* – that; *kabhu nahe* – never; *anitya* – temporary; *vaibhava* – opulence; *se* – that; *hari-sambandha* – is related to Lord Hari; *śunya* – free from; *māyāgandha* – tinge of illusion; *tāhā* – that; *kabhu naya* – is never; *jaḍera kaitava* – material hypocrisy.

Translation

Vaishnava qualities are attractive to everyone, so pure devotees become famous. However, their name and fame is not a temporary material opulence but eternal. Because it is related to Lord

Hari, it's free from any tinge of material illusion. It is not at all material hypocrisy.

Commentary

Vaishnava qualities such as being as humble as a blade of grass, as tolerant as a tree, and completely free from the desire for material name, worship, and gain, as well as the willingness to give all due respect to everyone else and chanting the holy names of the Lord, are attractive, so it's natural that Vaishnavas attract name and fame. However, name and fame in this sense are not material opulences but a manifestation of the Lord's opulence. Since whatever is connected with the Lord is eternal, there is no question of this type of name and fame being destructive. My previous teachers, His Divine Grace Srila Bhakti Pramode Puri Goswami Thakur, His Divine Grace Srila Prabhupada Bhaktisiddhanta Saraswati Thakur, His Divine Grace Srila Gour Kishore Das Babaji Maharaj, His Divine Grace Srila Bhaktivinode Thakur, His Divine Grace Srila Jagannath Das Babaji Maharaj, His Divine Grace Srila Baladeva

Vidyabhushan, His Divine Grace Srila Vishvanath Chakravarti Thakur, His Divine Grace Srila Narottama Das Thakur, His Divine Grace Srila Shrinivas Acharya, His Divine Grace Srila Shyamananda Pandit, His Divine Grace Srila Krishnadas Kaviraj Goswami, His Divine Grace Srila Vrindavan Das Thakur, Prabhupada Srila Rupa Goswami, Prabhupada Srila Sanatana Goswami, Prabhupada Srila Jiva Goswami, Prabhupada Srila Raghunath Bhatta Goswami, Prabhupada Srila Gopal Bhatta Goswami, Prabhupada Srila Raghunath Das Goswami, and others, are all eternally famous. They are not famous because of their material opulence. Their fame is due to their devotional wealth and for embodying the above Vaishnava qualities.

Whoever has even a little connection with Vaishnavism worships all these personalities, and by their blessings develops the abovementioned Vaishnava qualities. Only by the blessings of our previous teachers are we able to establish our eternal relationship with Lord Hari and attain Vaishnava qualities. Whomever has their blessings will automatically have a relationship with Lord Hari. Such persons will be completely free from any tinge of material attachment and will be renowned. They will attain name and fame without any tinge of material illusion – meaning, their attainment will be entirely spiritual. Such individuals are not hypocrites, making a show of humility, but are naturally endowed with Vaishnava qualities and have achieved the goal of their spiritual practice.

Vaishnava spiritual practice is based on *anugatya,* or following in the footsteps of the previous teachers. If anyone is inventing processes out of their own mind, then outwardly, such persons may get name and fame by hypocritically presenting themselves as if they have Vaishnava qualities, but in reality they have failed to achieve the ultimate goal of life. In order to achieve our ultimate goal of entering the abode of the Supreme Lord to perform eternal service according to our eternal age and in our eternal dress and form, we need to surrender and become completely free of hypocrisy. Surrender means to follow in the footsteps of the previous teachers (*anugatya*).

Text 6

pratiṣṭhā-caṇḍālī, nirjanatā-jāli,
ubhaye jāniha māyika raurava
'kīrtana-chāḍiba, pratiṣṭhā mākhiba'
ki kāja ḍhuṅḍiyā tādṛśa gaurava

Word-for-word

pratiṣṭhā – material name and fame; *caṇḍālī* – demonic motivation; *nirjanatā* – solitude; *jāli* – netlike trap; *ubhaye* – in both; *jāniha* – know; *māyika raurava* – hell of illusion; *kīrtana* – congregationally chanting the holy names of Lord Hari; *chāḍiba* – I will give it up; *pratiṣṭhā* – material name and fame; *mākhiba* – I will smear on myself; *ki* – what; *kāja* – work; *ḍhuṅḍiyā* – searching for; *tādṛśa* – like that; *gaurava* – material respect and opulence.

Translation

You should know that both the demonic motivation for material name and fame and the netlike trap of isolation are like the hell of illusion called *raurava*. What business do you have searching for mundane respect born from expressing, "I will give up congregationally chanting the Lord's holy names and instead opt for the pretense of solitary worship, smearing material name and fame on myself"?

Commentary

The majority of people are blinded by their desire for material name and fame and thus are unable to see anything, be it good or bad. For example, a number of flowers are known for their fragrance, but on some occasions, the center of these flowers is infested with insects. Attracted by the fragrance of the flowers, a blind man may try to catch a closer whiff, holding the flower close to his nose. Because he is blind he doesn't recognize the infestation. So rather than experiencing the intensified fragrance exuding from the flower's center he feels pain as he draws the bugs into his nose. Distress is inevitable for materialists blinded by the desire for material name and fame. Furthermore, in order to achieve that mundane respect, these persons even cheat and kill and act in all kinds of other harmful ways in order to fulfill their ambitions. Pure devotees consider such tendencies and motivations demonic (*chandali*).

It has become common for unscrupulous persons, in the name of chanting the holy names, to find a solitary place to sit and chant. Under false pretenses they then present themselves to the public as spiritually elevated *sadhus* who are free from material desires. They use these tactics to achieve material name, fame, and wealth as well as to attract followers. Such pretenders usually attract materialists seeking to relieve themselves of the sins accrued by their materialistic activities. It is said, "Birds of a feather flock together." These insincere, solitary chanters provide a classic example of the nature of this age of hypocrisy. Instead of serving the Lord under the guidance of their previous teachers, they prefer to stay alone in a holy land, completely neglecting *anugatya* and shamelessly cheating the Lord, themselves, and anyone who follows them.

Usually, materialists make their money by performing sinful activities. In order to free themselves from the reactions of their sins they donate a portion of their wealth to these pretenders and, applying their materialistic intelligence for gain, make a show of themselves being spiritually advanced and free from the desire for mundane name and fame. However, they are only after public recognition. At the end of the day, both are cheated and will be trapped in the hellish net of material illusion.

When people chant and sing the holy names to please the public's senses in order to gain appreciation and recognition for themselves instead of expanding the Lord's fame (*loka-ranjana*), they certainly miss the essence of spiritual practice. Gaining public appreciation in itself doesn't allow us to attain the ultimate goal of life, Goloka Vrindavan. What's the use of seeking mundane respect at the cost of losing the value of one's human life?

The pure devotees' goal in chanting is solely to please the Lord. When we veer from that goal, we are most definitely trapped in illusion, which gradually drags us into a hellish condition. Material name, fame, and gain are all temporary prizes. People may appreciate us today, but tomorrow they may reject or deceive us. That's the nature of the material world. Therefore, magnanimous spirituality teaches us not to chase material name, fame, distinction, worship, and other material assets. Rather, we learn to pray to the Lord for the association of pure devotees and to be allowed to follow in their footsteps. Vaishnava association will indeed allow us to enter the eternal, blissful, peaceful abode of the Supreme Lord.

In this verse Srila Prabhupada Bhaktisiddhanta Saraswati Thakur instructs us to apply our intelligence. He teaches us that instead of chasing material opulence we should desire the association of pure devotees who are eligible to give us the Lord's mercy, the goal of human life.

Text 7

mādhavendra purī, bhāvaghare curi,
nā karila kabhu sadāi jānaba
tomāra pratiṣṭhā, – 'śūkarera viṣṭhā'
tāra saha sama kabhu nā mānaba

Word-for-word

mādhavendra purī – Madhavendra Puri; *bhāvaghare curi* – making a show of experiencing spiritual ecstasies; *nā karila kabhu* – never did; *sadāi* – always; *jānaba* – I will know; *tomāra* – your; *pratiṣṭhā* – material name and fame; *śūkarera viṣṭhā* – stool of a hog; *tāra saha sama* – equal to him; *kabhu nā mānaba* – I will never accept.

Translation

We must know that Madhavendra Puripada's devotional mood was not at all material. His ecstasy was completely natural, and he never made a show of experiencing spiritual ecstasies in order to gain material respect. However, your tendency to want material name, fame, and gain is like the stool of a hog. We can never consider your materialistic name and fame comparable to the name and fame won by Madhavendra Puripada.

Commentary

Madhavendra Puripada is a noteworthy teacher in our lineage. He is the spiritual master of both Advaita Acharya and Ishvara Puri. Lord Krishna manifested an attractive pastime with Madhavendra Puripada to help us understand the devotional attachment between the Lord and His devotees.

Once, Madhavendra Puri went to Vrindavan, vowing not to beg even for his food. He also vowed that even if someone wanted to give him food, he would drink only milk, and that, too, only if someone spontaneously offered it to him. One evening, while Madhavendra Puripada was sitting under a tree at Govinda Kund, near Govardhan Hill, and joyfully chanting the Lord's name, a cowherd boy approached him with a pot of milk, saying, "You must be hungry. You haven't eaten all day. Please drink this milk."

Madhavendra Puri noticed the boy's beautiful,

attractive features and gentle nature, and he asked, "How do you know I haven't eaten?"

The boy replied, "I was told by a housewife, who saw you sitting here. She gave Me this pot of milk for you. Please drink it. Keep the pot. I will come back for it later."

Madhavendra Puripada drank the milk, which was as fragrant as a lotus and tasted like nectar. The boy didn't reveal His true identity to Madhavendra Puri, but He was none other than the Supreme Person, Sri Krishna. However, Madhavendra Puri only realized this fact once he had consumed the extraordinary milk. He thought, "When the boy comes to collect the pot I will catch Him!"

Madhavendra Puri waited a long time, but the boy never returned. Eventually, Madhavendra Puri drowsed and fell asleep. The boy appeared in his dream. Instead of Madhavendra Puri catching the boy, the boy caught Madhavendra Puri's hand and pulled him toward a jungle on the side of Govardhan Hill, saying, "Afraid of the Muslim ruler, My devotees hid Me here. I've been suffering for days, staying here in my deity form, exposed to the hot sun and rain. I have been waiting for you to come. Please go to the surrounding villages and ask the men to cut through the jungle so you can find Me. Then reinstall Me." Thus the dream ended.

Madhavendra Puripada rose and told the villagers about his dream. Full of enthusiasm the villagers went with Madhavendra Puripada to the jungle, where they eventually found the deity of Lord Gopal holding Govardhan Hill in His left hand.

Madhavendra Puri reinstalled Gopal at the top of Govardhan Hill and performed a grand bathing ceremony. After the ceremony, Gopal again visited him in a dream, this time saying, "Although you performed all the ceremonies, the heat in My body was not relieved. Please go south and bring sandalwood (*malayaja chandan*) to cool Me."

Madhavendra Puri was aged at the time, but on hearing the Lord's order he gave no thought to his physical condition or the difficulties of such a long journey. And because of his surrender, the Lord empowered him to walk south from Vrindavan.

On the way, he passed through Remuna, where there is an ancient Gopinath temple. This temple has a tradition of offering twelve bowls of *amritakeli* (sweet rice) to Gopinath each evening. While visiting the temple and taking darshan of the deities, Madhavendra Puripada saw the priest offering the twelve bowls of sweet rice. Madhavendra Puripada desired to taste the sweet rice, thinking that if he did, he would be able to prepare the same offering for his Gopal. But he instantly reproached himself; after all, he had taken a vow to beg for nothing and to only accept donated milk. Feeling ashamed, he left the temple and went to a deserted marketplace, where he sat to chant.

At midnight, in order to fulfill Madhavendra Puri's desire, Gopinath appeared in the dream of His priest, saying, "I have hidden a bowl of sweet rice inside the temple. Please bathe and enter the temple, find the sweet rice, and take it to Madhavendra Puri, who is chanting at that deserted marketplace."

Here we can see that the Lord stole a bowl of sweet rice to fulfill the desire of Madhavendra Puri. How affectionate the Lord is toward His devotees, especially when He reciprocates with their loving devotion. If we were the subject of such a theft, we would probably advertise it publicly, promoting our ability to please the Lord and making a show of our gravity or good fortune to prove how exalted we are. However, instead of showing off his devotion, Madhavendra Puri became fearful of the fame that would follow this demonstration of the Lord's mercy and left the place.

As soon as the priest gave Madhavendra Puri the sweet rice, Madhavendra ate it and, at sunrise, ran away. Although this was a wonderful act by the Lord in every sense – many would consider it a miracle – Madhavendra Puri never used it to promote himself. Rather, he tried his best to hide what had happened. Madhavendra Puripada's mood is the actual mood of devotion, which is completely free from the desire for material worship, name, gain, and fame. Madhavendra Puripada's finding the Gopal deity, and Gopinath stealing sweet rice for His devotee, are not myths but devotional facts.

According to Krishnadas Kaviraj Goswamipada, Madhavendra Puri was the first person to realize Radharani's mood of separation from Krishna. After Madhavendra Puri, such a mood of separation was found only in Sri Chaitanya Mahaprabhu, the combined form of Radha and

Krishna. There is no fourth person where this mood of separation is found.

The manifestation of this topmost separation was first experienced by Srimati Radharani, who is nondifferent from Krishna and who is the Lord's pleasure-giving potency. One time, Krishna and His elder brother, Balaram, were invited by their uncle, Kamsa, to go to Mathura. Krishna and Balaram mounted the chariot and prepared to leave, but Radharani and Her *sakhīs* (associates) blocked the chariot's path and manifested their first expression of separation. At that time Krishna vowed to Radharani and Her *sakhis* that He would return to Vrindavan very soon. Much time passed, but Krishna never returned. He still has not come back to Vrindavan. Separation born from Krishna's physical absence caused Radharani to lament:

ayi dīna dayārdra nātha he mathurā-nātha kadāvalokyase hṛdayaṁ tvad-aloka kātaram dayita bhrāmyati kiṁ karomyaham.

ayi – O; *dīna-dayārdra-nātha* – master who is compassionate on the fallen; *he* – O; *mathurā-nātha* – master of Mathura; *kadāvalokyase* – when will I be able to see you; *hṛdayam* – heart; *tvad-aloka kātaram* – pain from not seeing You; *dayita* – O my dear; *bhrāmyati* – becomes overwhelmed; *kim* – what; *karomyaham* – do I do.

"O deliverer of the fallen souls! You are the Lord of Vrindavan, but now You have become the Lord of Mathura." Krishna, from the core of His heart, stays always in Vrindavan. However, being extremely afflicted by the pain of separation, Srimati Radharani says, "O Lord of Mathura!" Then at the next moment She says, "My heart is leaping from My chest because I so much desire to personally serve You." This internal expression of deep, intense love coupled with Her external expression of anger is called *maan,* or sulkiness. Under the influence of *maan* Srimati Radharani continues, "My dear, without this service to You, what will I do?"

Seeing the highest manifestation of the feelings of separation, Srila Krishnadas Kaviraj Goswamipada made the following known to us:

ei śloka kahiyāchena rādhā-ṭhākurāṇī
tāṅra kṛpāya sphuriyāche mādhavendra-vāṇī
kibā gauracandra ihā kare āsvādana
ihā āsvādite āra nāhi cauṭha-jana
(Chaitanya-charitamrita)

ei – this; *śloka* – verse; *kahiyāchena* – has spoken; *rādhā-ṭhākurāṇī* – Radharani, who is the supreme controller; *tāṅra* – Her; *kṛpaya* – by the mercy; *sphuriyāche* – has manifested; *mādhavendra-vāṇī* – the words of Madhavendra Puri; *kibā* – what; *gauracandra* – Gaurachandra; *ihā* – here; *kare āsvādana* – tastes; *ihā* – here; *āsvādite* – to taste; *āra nāhi* – no other; *cauṭha-jana* – fourth person.

"This verse [*ayi dina-dayardra-natha*] was spoken by Srimati Radha Thakurani. By Her mercy, this verse was manifested through the words of Madhavendra Puri. Sri Gaurachandra tasted this verse. There is no fourth person who can taste it."

By studying the above two verses we can understand that, first, Srimati Radharani uttered this topmost expression of separation, *ayi dina-dayardra-natha*, with the objective of getting the Supreme Personality of Godhead, Sri Krishna, to return to Vrindavan. After being tasted by Her, this topmost expression of separation was tasted by the *acharya* of divine love, Madhavendra Puripada, for whom both Advaita Acharya and Nityananda Prabhu had utmost respect, reverence, and affection. After being tasted by Madhavendra Puri, this topmost feeling of separation was tasted by Sri Shachinandana Gaurahari, who is

Sri Krishna Himself beautifully ornamented with Radharani's mood and complexion. Gaurahari is the form of extreme magnanimity, coming to deliver everyone in this iron age of Kali, and He is the life of the residents of Nadia. At last, Srila Krishnadas Kaviraj Goswami writes that other than these three divine personalities – Srimati Radharani, Sri Madhavendra Puripada, and Sri Gaurahari – to this day there is no fourth person in the entire community of devotees who can taste the mood of separation this verse speaks of.

There is not even a tinge of material enjoyment in Madhavendra Puripada's devotional ecstasies. Many people pretend to have such devotional moods in order to get material name, fame, worship, and distinction – a tendency that's comparable to hog stool. I have seen hogs eat all the dirt created by others. How dirty, then, is the hog's stool? It is incredibly dirty. We cannot equate such dirtiness with any other contaminated substance in the material world. Otherwise, why did His Divine Grace Srila Bhaktisiddhanta Prabhupada say so?

In our Vaishnava tradition it is mentioned that there are six enemies in the heart: lust, anger, greed, material infatuation, madness, and envy. A devotional practitioner is capable of controlling the first five enemies by engaging them in the Lord's service. The sixth enemy, envy, cannot be conquered by dovetailing it in the Lord's service. When people become envious they have a tendency to want material name, fame, and distinction. My spiritual master, His Divine Grace Srila Bhakti Pramode Puri Goswami Thakur, often called envy the final enemy that remains stuck deep within the heart. Envy provides Mayadevi with her final whip (*chabuka*), which she uses to drive us to try for material popularity. Envy is difficult for any spiritual practitioner to overcome until that practitioner receives mercy from our *parampara*. Without such mercy it is impossible to give up envy.

All other material tendencies are born of envy. Envy is stuck in our hearts in a dry form. When we engage our energy in trying to become popular, we cannot attain the goal of spiritual life. Persons are eligible to reach their spiritual goal when they become completely free of all material attachment.

Text 8

matsaratā-vaśe, tumi jaḍarase,
majecha chāḍiyā kīrtana-sauṣṭhava
tāi duṣṭa mana, 'nirjana-bhajana',
pracāricha chale 'kuyogī-vaibhava'

Word-for-word

matsaratā – envy; *vaśe* – under the control of; *tumi* – you; *jaḍarase* – taste of material mellows of name, fame, and worship; *majecha* – intoxicated; *chāḍiyā* – giving up; *kīrtana* – congregational chanting; *sauṣṭhava* – beauty; *tāi* – therefore; *duṣṭa* – wicked; *mana* – mind; *nirjana-bhajana* – solitary spiritual practice; *pracāricha* – showing; *chale* – deceptive pretense; *kuyogī* – a spiritual practitioner on the wrong path; *vaibhava* – material recognition.

Translation

You are drowning in the mellows of material name, fame, and worship because you are completely under the control of envy. You have given up the beauty of congregationally chanting the holy names. Thus, O wicked mind, all your pretense of sitting in solitary spiritual practice is just a means for you to gain material recognition. It is the characteristic of a spiritual practitioner on the wrong path.

Commentary

Envy is such a dirty tendency that it cannot be engaged in any type of service for the Supreme Lord. In the *Mahabharata* we see how Duryodhana, the eldest son of Dhritarashtra and Gandhari, embodied envy. He neither externally nor internally appreciated the honesty, simplicity, or magnanimity of the Pandavas. Even the Supreme Lord is attracted to those qualities, but Duryodhana, being intoxicated by envy, never appreciated the Pandavas. Yudhishthira Maharaj was the rightful heir to the throne at Hastinapur and was appointed to rule. Despite this, however, Duryodhana wanted the throne for himself. To get it, Duryodhana conspired to kill the Pandava brothers along with their mother Kuntidevi, who was his own aunt. With these evil plans in mind, Duryodhana approached Yudhishthira Maharaj in a sweet way and asked the Pandavas to go on pilgrimage. He wanted to rid himself of them once and for all, and so, in a ploy to destroy them while they were sleeping, he had a beautiful palace constructed for them and coated with an ignitable wax. Duryodhana and the Pandavas were cousins, but envy brought down Duryodhana's consciousness and contaminated his mind to such a wicked extent that he was ready to kill his cousins in a manner so violent as to burn them in their beds.

I have already mentioned the six enemies in the heart, namely lust, anger, greed, illusion, madness, and envy. Now I will briefly explain their harmful effects and how, other than envy, each of them can be engaged in the Lord's service.

Kama: Lust is commonly defined as a strong sexual desire between man and woman, which is usually a purely selfish, sensual pleasure, and which usually leads to illicit connections. If, however, a spiritual practitioner sincerely uses lust to conceive a child who will serve the Lord, then lust can be dovetailed.

Krodha: Some people have angry dispositions. When we use anger to satisfy our own motives, it only destroys our intelligence and harms society. If instead we use anger to rectify others rather than harm them, then anger becomes service to the Lord. Anger can also be used to protect the Lord's devotees from offensive persons, especially from people who blaspheme devotees. When we use anger to stop a person from blaspheming devotees, that anger is considered pleasing to the Lord, and it also protects the blasphemer from committing further offenses toward the devotees.

Lobha: People will go to extreme lengths and commit atrocities to satisfy their greed. Greed only forces us to commit actions that accrue bad karma. Bad karmic actions pull us down into intense suffering – so intense that most people would feel they were in hell. Nonetheless, we can develop intense greed for hearing the glories of the Supreme Lord from bona fide spiritual practitioners and follow in their footsteps in order to uplift ourselves rather than accumulating more and more material name, fame, and gain. In this way, greed can be engaged to please the Lord.

Moha: To be in illusion means to accept something that is not true as true. False ego and the Lord's illusory potency make us think our bodies are our selves. According to the Vaishnava philosophy, this idea is considered an illusion. Actually, we are the soul, eternal servants of the Supreme Lord, but somehow we have accepted a temporary material body as our true identity and think we have no connection to or relationship with God. The result of remaining in such illusion is that we can never really experience the happiness we deserve. Instead, life after life we succumb to various unpleasant situations. Although the body and everything in this world form part of the Lord's illusory energy, everything can still be used in His service. Our bodies have a number of faculties, such as speech, hearing, the ability to use our hands and legs, and so forth – and all of them can be used to serve the Lord. For example, we can use our voice to glorify and sing for the Lord, our hands to clean the Lord's temple, our legs to visit places of pilgrimage where the Lord has had pastimes. Although this world and our present material body are both products of illusion, when those same products of illusion are used to glorify Sri Krishna, they purify the soul. In this manner, the soul eventually attains its loving relationship with Sri Krishna and becomes free from the illusory entanglement of this material world.

Mada: When people are blind and mad for material gain, we call it *mada*, "madness." When we use the tendency for madness to become completely infatuated with serving the Lord and His devotees, then madness yields an abundance of spiritual gain instead of destroying our physical, mental, and emotional health. When people are materially mad for selfish gains, it creates disharmony and dissatisfaction, but when we engage madness in serving the Lord and His devotees, it has the opposite effect. Madness in this world brings about destruction, yet if we use it to chant the holy names of God as taught by Lord Chaitanya, who is none other than Krishna Himself, it restores equilibrium and unites everyone. The power invested in the sound vibration of the holy names can free human beings from their miserable material existence, and this power is not only limited to humans but extends to all other living beings, even those who may not be able to chant. To become free from our miserable condition we have to become mad after chanting the holy names of God. Chaitanya Mahaprabhu's followers became mad after chanting the holy names. That madness after, or infatuation with, chanting the holy names is beneficial to the chanter and a service to all living beings, and it ultimately pleases the Lord in every respect.

Matsarya: Envy cannot be used to serve the Lord. Envy is a quality of the material realm, and it cannot be transformed and then used in a spiritual act. Envy brings only suffering and causes us to take birth in various species of life, becoming trapped in the cycle of repeated birth and death (*samsara*). Duryodhana was the perfect example of someone who was envious in his dealings but ultimately faced a gruesome end along with all his family members.

When a human being is hypocritical, that person may take birth in his or her next life as a poisonous snake deep in the jungle. We should avoid hypocrisy by not making a show of solitary spiritual practice while desiring material gain. We should not give up the beauty of wholeheartedly and congregationally chanting the holy names under the guidance of the teachers in our *parampara*. Hypocrisy definitely draws suffering to us. Rather, wholeheartedly following in the footsteps of our previous teachers will lead us toward spiritual bliss in the eternal service of the Divine Couple, Sri Sri Radha and Krishna. This service is the main goal to be achieved while in the human form. Thus, O mind, do not engage in wicked tendencies that are self-deceiving and make you forgetful of your true identity. Hypocrites also mislead society.

The main goal of genuine spiritual practitioners who are chanting the holy names is to clean the dirt of the desire for material name, fame, and gain from their hearts. Gradually, they become detached from all material attachment and, as a result, the doors to the eternal abode are made accessible to them so that they can eternally serve the Lord and live a blissful life.

In this verse, Srila Prabhupada Bhaktisiddhanta Saraswati Thakur warns his followers not to engage in any kind of deceit in order to gain material recognition. Nowadays, we see that many people pretend to be following in the footsteps of Prabhupada Bhaktisiddhanta, choosing a solitary place to chant, especially near Govinda Kund at Govardhana, as well as in various places around *dhamas* like Navadvipa, Puri, and Vraja Mandala. They indulge their laziness and enjoy the recognition they get from the various pilgrims.

However, I would like to point out that not all those who practice solitary chanting, as Prabhupada did, to become pure enough to spread the loving mission of Sri Chaitanya Mahaprabhu, are charlatans. However, apart from these rare few genuine personalities, most are only making a show of exalted spiritual practice for their own personal gain. Prabhupada Bhaktisiddhanta Saraswati Thakur repeatedly instructed us not to engage in such activities, particularly indulging in laziness or other forms of deceit.

Text 9

prabhu sanātane parama yatane,
śikṣā dila yāhā, cinta sei saba
sei du'ṭī kathā, bhula' nā sarvathā,
uccaiḥsvare kara 'harināma-raba'

Word-for-word

prabhu – Mahaprabhu; *sanātane* – Sanatana Goswami, one of the great teachers in the Gaudiya Vaishnava lineage; *parama* – utmost; *yatane* – care; *śikṣā* – teachings; *dila* – gave; *yāhā* – that which; *cinta* – think about; *sei* – that; *saba* – all; *sei* – that; *du'ṭī* – two; *kathā* – instructions; *bhula'* – forget; *nā* – not; *sarvathā* – always in all circumstances; *uccaiḥsvare* – in a loud voice; *kara* – do; *harināma-raba* – resounding chanting of the holy names.

Translation

Think about all of the teachings that Caitanya Mahāprabhu personally gave Sanātana Gosvāmī and carefully apply them in your lives. Never forget the two instructions that Mahāprabhu gave to Sanātana Gosvāmī when he asked, "Who am I?" and "Why am I suffering?". Fill the world with the loud, resounding chanting of the holy names.

Commentary

Lord Chaitanya Mahaprabhu appeared with His associates in this material world in order to freely distribute divine love without discrimination. The wealth of divine love from the Lord's eternal abode appeared here in this material world in the form of the Hare Krishna *maha-mantra*. Although Mahaprabhu freely distributes the wealth of divine love, He also teaches surrender to the *parampara*, without hypocrisy. This is the process by which we gain complete access to His magnanimous mercy, as surrender (*sharanagati*) is the life and soul of devotional practice.

It has been stated in the Gaudiya history that Sanatana Goswami is eternally Lavanga Manjari in the spiritual world. Lord Chaitanya brought Lavanga Manjari into the material world during His pastimes for the purpose of establishing conclusive devotional principles. In this regard, I will give you a brief description of Sanatana Goswami's life.

Sanatana Goswami was born in a *brahmana* family. His birth name was Santosh. He was the elder brother of Amara, who was later known as Rupa Goswami. Both brothers exhibited extreme intelligence. They previously lived in a village called Ramakeli, in present-day Malda district, West Bengal. During that time, the region was under the Muslim rule of Hussain Shah.

Once, Hussain Shah decided to build a mosque. When the construction was almost finished, he went to the top of the dome with the chief mason. For some reason, the mason told Hussain Shah that he could have made the mosque even more beautiful. Hearing this made Hussain Shah angry because he had wanted to build the most beautiful mosque, and without any recourse to the law he pushed the mason from the dome to his death. When Hussain Shah came down to the ground, he saw one of his employees nearby and ordered him to go to a village named Marga. The employee didn't understand Hussain Shah's purpose in sending him there, but he left for the village and, on the way, arrived in Ramakeli. There, he saw two boys studying on the path. Still confused about the purpose of his trip, the employee began to pace not far from these boys. The boys were Santosh and Amara. Trying to understand the employee's anxiety, the boys called him over, and the employee narrated the whole incident between Hussain Shah and the mason and the order he had subsequently received. Understanding Hussain Shah's intention, the two boys asked the employee to find several masons who could be brought before the king.

The employee did so quickly, and when he returned to the king, Hussain Shah remarked, "I didn't tell you why I sent you to that village. How did you know my desire so exactly?" The employee replied, "This was not due to my own intelligence. I met two boys in Ramakeli, and they told me to send these masons to you." Impressed by the boys' intelligence and understanding their potential, Hussain Shah ordered the employee to bring the boys to him. As soon as the boys arrived, Hussain Shah appointed Santosh the kingdom's prime minister and Amara its finance minister. Their names were also changed. Santosh became Sakara Mallik and Amara became Dabir Khasa.

All living beings are originally the Lord's

eternal servants. By hearing the life histories of Haridas Thakur, Rupa Goswami, and Sanatana Goswami, we can understand how Lord Chaitanya distributed the treasure of divine love without discrimination of caste or creed. Haridas Thakur, who was originally Lord Brahma, was born in a Muslim family; Rupa and Sanatana were connected with Hussain Shah as ministers and became Muslims under his rule. Even though these three personalities were Muslims, the Lord demonstrated that His mercy is beyond caste and creed; He used them as examples in order to fulfill His will.

Eventually, Sanatana Goswami left his post in Hussain Shah's kingdom and made his way toward Kashi. Although learned, in order to teach the whole world and to fulfill the will of the Lord, Sanatana Goswami took the role of a naive student and asked the following questions to Lord Chaitanya at Kashi Varanasi:

ke āmī kene āmāya jāre tāpa-traya
ihā nāhi jāni kemane hita haya

"Who am I? Why am I forced to be burned by the threefold miseries (*tri-tapa*) of material existence, caused by body and mind (*adhyatmika*), other living entities (*adhibhautika*), and higher living entities, who cause natural calamities (*adhidaivika*)?

sādhya-sādhana-tattva puchite nā jāni
kṛpā kari' saba tattva kaha ta' āpani

"I don't know how to inquire about the practice of spirituality and the goal of practicing it (*sadhya-sadhana-tattva*). Please mercifully instruct me on everything that I should know and do."

Mahaprabhu replied:

jīvera svarūpa haya kṛṣṇera nitya dāsa
kṛṣṇera taṭasthā-śakti bhedābheda-prakāśa

"All living entities are constitutionally eternal servants of Lord Krishna. They are the Lord's marginal potency, meaning they can be influenced by both the material and spiritual natures." Just as sparks emanate constantly from a blazing fire, so the *jivatmas* (souls) constantly emanate from the blazing fire that is the Paramatma (Supersoul). Both the *jivatma* and the Paramatma are the same in quality (*abheda*) in that they are both spiritual by nature. However, the Supreme Lord is always eternally situated in the spiritual energy, whereas the *jivatma* can come under the influence of the material energy. When under the control of the material energy, the *jivatma* must undergo many changes, including being embodied in various forms, sometimes as a human being, sometimes as an animal, sometimes as a demigod, and sometimes as one of the other 8,400,000 types of bodies. It is the tendency to fall into the material energy that makes the *jivatma* and the Paramatma different (*bheda*).

We should always be aware of our eternal constitutional position and our purpose when in the human form. Our ultimate goal is to establish our eternal constitutional position as eternal servants of Krishna. Due to the influence of the illusory energy, we forget our constitutional position, and by the influence of the association we receive in this world, we find ourselves situated in a variety of material designations. When we study, we think ourselves students. After completing our studies, we identify ourselves with our respective occupations – perhaps we're lawyers or doctors or teachers. Eventually, we marry and identify ourselves as spouses, and then parents and then grandparents. Ultimately, we die, still ignorant of our eternal constitutional position.

In this verse, His Divine Grace Srila Prabhupada Bhaktisiddhanta Saraswati Thakur is instructing us to be careful not to forget our eternal constitutional position at any step of our lives. He also emphatically requests us to loudly and wholeheartedly chant the Hare Krishna *maha-mantra.* In order to destroy all the material attachments that we have accumulated through our material association, Srila Prabhupada again instructs us to resoundingly chant the holy names in a mood of surrender, with no tinge of hypocrisy.

Text 10

'phalgu' āra 'yukta' 'baddha' āra 'mukta',
kabhu nā bhāviba ekākāra saba
'kanaka-kāminī, 'pratiṣṭhā-bāghinī',
chāḍiyāche yāre sei ta' vaiṣṇava

Word-for-word

phalgu – fake; *āra* – and; *yukta* – attentively connected; *baddha* – materially attached and bound; *āra* – and; *mukta* – free from material attachment; *kabhu nā* – never; *bhāviba* – think; *ekākāra* – one and the same; *saba* – all; *kanaka* – money and material wealth; *kāminī* – women (or sensual desire); *pratiṣṭhā* – material name and fame; *bāghinī* – tigress; *chāḍiyāche* – has left; *yāre* – whom; *sei* – that person; *ta'* – is certainly considered; *vaiṣṇava* – pure devotee.

Translation

We should not think that one who is attentively practicing spirituality is the same as one who pretends to practice spirituality. Similarly, we should not consider a person who is materially attached to be the same as a person who is free from material attachment. A person completely free of attachment to material wealth, sensual desire, and the tigress of material name and fame is considered a pure devotee.

Commentary

The word *phalgu* is significant here. There is a river in Gaya, Bihar, called the Phalgu. If one goes there, one will see that there is no water in the riverbed. However, if one digs into the sand a little, one will find water. Similarly, people pretend to have an attachment to their spiritual practice, but internally their practice is not actually motivated by a desire to become free of material attachment; rather, they want to become more and more attached to name, fame, gain, and recognition. We have seen how externally, political leaders make a show of generosity in the name of helping their citizens, but their real goal is different from what they are showing us. Like mirages in the desert, from afar they promise us that there is water to drink, but unfortunately, the closer we get to it the more we realize we've been tricked. Such duplicity is called *phalgu*, and it is completely prohibited in both spiritual and material endeavors.

In the material world truth always comes to us in a roundabout or zigzag manner. Today we may cheat someone, but tomorrow the truth will come out and we will be exposed. There's a famous statement by Abraham Lincoln: "You can fool some of the people all of the time, and all of the people some of the time, but you cannot fool all of the people all of the time." Vaishnava spiritual practice is based only on absolute truth. Therefore, our tradition never appreciates *phalgu* tendencies. Any sincere person who is searching for the highest goal of human life should try to remain as far as possible from the tendency to be false. Otherwise, all our endeavors in spiritual practice will yield only trouble and never bear the real fruit due a genuine spiritual practitioner.

Of all the species in this world, humans have been gifted with superior intelligence. In most circumstances, human beings do not live more than one hundred years. Within these one hundred years, according to the calculation of our previous teachers, we spend half our lives sleeping. We spend more than fifteen years as children and in sickness, and in our youth we spend most of our energy trying to fulfill our sense desires. When we reach old age, although we understand that we've spent many years wasting time, it's unfortunately too late to sincerely engage in spiritual practice because of our physical and mental condition. As soon as someone hears from a pure devotee of the ultimate goal of life and sincerely engages in spiritual practice, he or she is considered very fortunate (*bhagyavan*). When people are materially attached and have an offensive mentality, they are considered to be *baddha,* materially bound. Their practice will not deliver them to the spiritual world. Rather, their offensive tendencies will pull them down again and again into the material world.

As far as we can see these days, people consider those who are very materially attached, accumulating lots of material wealth, name, fame, and recognition, to be extremely lucky. But those with spiritual vision consider a person who is free from all material attachment and who is fully connected to God at every step to be truly lucky.

Please don't think that those who are materially

wealthy cannot become devotees. Material wealth is not bad in itself; it is the *attachment* to material wealth that is bad. For example, most people consider money their second God. But money is not God. Still, that doesn't mean money is bad. Money can be bad based on how we use it. Similarly, when we realize that everything belongs to the Lord, then we see ourselves as caretakers of the Lord's property; in this sense, property is not bad. It's the same if we use our studies, employment, marriage, progeny, and every phase of life in the service of the Lord purely for His satisfaction – we are engaging in spiritual practice at every step of our lives. The point is that everything in this world and all the phases of lives are meant for the Lord's service and for His satisfaction.

Please think about King Ambarish from *Srimad-Bhagavatam* and King Prataparudra from the time of Mahaprabhu. Although we know that kings are generally materialists, these two kings never thought that their wealth and kingdoms belonged to them. Rather, they always considered themselves caretakers of the Lord's property. Thus we consider these apparently materialistic persons as attentive practitioners of spirituality in service to the Lord.

We shouldn't think that materially wealthy people are always bound by material attachment. All the previous teachers in our line (*mahajanas*) engaged each of their activities in glorifying the Lord and following in the footsteps of the Lord and His pure devotees. When we make our best attempt to follow in the footsteps of our previous teachers, we are considered *yukta*, "connected" to the Lord. The Lord's mercy will then come down to us through our previous teachers, our current gurus, and the Vaishnavas. If there's no sincere connection with our teachers and other Vaishnavas, we won't be eligible for the Lord's mercy – not even through pretense. We should therefore not consider pretenders and genuine practitioners to be one and the same.

Influenced by the Age of Kali, people are confused about the differences between pretenders and genuine spiritual practitioners. According to *shastra*, Vaishnava offenses increase our mundane attachments; so we can see that the offensive mentality society has toward Vaishnavas only increases people's desire for wealth and followers. And seeking wealth and followers side by side increases many people's offensive tendencies.

It's mentioned that we commit offenses

against the holy *dhama* when we conduct business there, collect money, and seek material wealth in the name of worshiping the deities and singing the holy names in *sankirtana*. Common people think that those who are materially wealthy and who have many followers are pure and advanced. These people also think that those who are sitting, chanting, and depending on begging are not pure and spiritually advanced simply because they are materially poor. Our previous teachers, such as Srila Bhaktivinode Thakur, Srila Gour Kishor Das Babaji Maharaj, Srila Jagannath Das Babaji Maharaj, Narottama Das Thakur, the Six Goswamis, and Lord Sri Krishna Chaitanya, never exemplified that purity requires having lots of mundane wealth and sycophantic followers. Rather, they preached the path of renunciation and intense spiritual practice. Intense spiritual practice requires fixing the mind on the Lord's eternal services in the spiritual world. Although physically we may be present in the material world, perhaps in a small room, and without money or followers, in spirit we shall eternally serve the Divine Couple in the spiritual world. This is the highly elevated spiritual state known as *turiya-bhava*.

The female tiger is attractive to the male tiger,

and despite all obstacles, the male tiger will inevitably run toward the female to enjoy its senses. Similarly, those who are intoxicated by their desire for material name, fame, recognition, and gain will not worry about the obstacles on their path. Prabhupada mentions that *pratishtha baghini,* the desire for material name, fame, distinction, and gain, is like that male tiger running to enjoy its senses.

In this verse, His Divine Grace Srila Prabhupada is trying to make us understand that those who are free from the propensity to accumulate wealth, experience sense enjoyment, and chase after name, fame, and recognition are to be considered pure Vaishnavas. Pure devotees never blaspheme anyone. We know from the third *shloka* of Mahaprabhu's *Shikshashtakam* that pure devotees are humbler than a blade of grass, are more tolerant than a tree, give respect to everyone, and expect no respect for themselves – and they constantly chant the holy names. These days we see people from different societies blaspheming one another on the internet, in books, and in other publications and media – all in the name of Vaishnava practice. In order to protect us from such pretenders Srila Prabhupada uses the terms *baddha* and *mukta*. Pretenders are materially bound (*baddha*); their activities are full of material attachments. Those who are free of material attachments, including the tendency to commit any type of offense, are considered free from the clutches of the material world and in the *mukta* state (liberated).

Text 11

sei 'anāsakta', sei 'śuddha-bhakta',
saṁsāra tathāya pāya parābhava
'yathāyogya-bhoga' nāhi tathā roga,
'anāsakta' sei, ki āra kahaba

Word-for-word

sei – that; *anāsakta* – free from material attachment; *sei* – that; *śuddha-bhakta* – pure devotee; *saṁsāra* – material cycle of birth and death; *tathāya* – therein; *pāya* – gets; *parābhava* – deliverance; *yathāyogya* – appropriate; *bhoga* – enjoyment; *nāhi* – no; *tathā* – there; *roga* – disease; *anāsakta* – free from material attachment; *sei* – that; *ki* – what; *āra* – more; *kahaba* – will say.

Translation

A person is considered a pure Vaishnava when he is completely free from all material attachment. Thus he gains deliverance from the material cycle of birth and death. When a pure devotee engages in only the necessary amount of sense enjoyment for the satisfaction of the Lord, he is not considered materially diseased, as he is completely free from material attachment. What more shall I say?

Commentary

In order to help you understand the real meaning of the word *anasakta*, "free from material attachment," I will tell you of Sri Chaitanya Mahaprabhu's teachings to Raghunath Das Goswami. Monkeys look renounced because they live in trees and eat only fruit. They don't even eat onions, garlic, or nonvegetarian foods, and they don't wear clothes. Despite these apparent signs of great renunciation, however, they are mischievous as soon as they get the opportunity. We see such mischievous monkeys near Seva-kunj in Vrindavan. If a pilgrim who wears glasses is inattentive for even a moment, the monkeys will steal his glasses. Then, as a business exchange, the monkey will demand food in return for the glasses. If the pilgrim doesn't give the food, the monkey will threaten to break the glasses in half. Furthermore, male monkeys keep many female monkeys to satisfy their senses. In this age people think renunciation means to act like these monkeys – monkey renunciation is called *markata-vairagya*. Actually, this is not renunciation at all. Through Raghunath Das Goswami, Mahaprabhu teaches:

markaṭa-vairāgya nā kara loka dekhāñā
yathā-yogya viṣaya bhuñja' anāsakta hañā
antare niṣṭhā kara, bāhye loka-vyavahāra
acirāt kṛṣṇa tomāya karibe uddhāra

"Don't act like a monkey, with its apparent renunciation, simply to show off for the public. Take only enough sense enjoyment so that you are able to serve. Remain materially detached. Internally, keep firm faith in serving the Lord while you perform each of your activities. Externally, perform all your material duties toward family, neighbors, and society. If you balance material duties with spiritual practices and don't harm others, Krishna will soon deliver you from your material bondage."

Sometimes, people think the word *samsara* applies only to those who are married; they think that those without families are automatically renounced. *Samsara* refers to the material cycle of birth and death. As long as we're attached to the material world we'll be forced to come back again and again, cycling through repeated birth and death in different forms according to our karma.

But being a pure devotee doesn't depend on whether you are a householder or a renunciant. According to Mahaprabhu, we are not here to be either enjoyers or renunciants but to realize our actual identity as servants. A servant's goal is to please his or her object of service. The object of service in our lineage is the Divine Couple, Sri Sri Radha-Krishna.

Householders have many responsibilities. They have to maintain their families by engaging in various occupations and professions. When all their apparently materialistic activities are performed solely to please the Lord, however, those activities become service to the Lord. So although such householders may seem very much attached to their families, because they perform all their duties and responsibilities to please the Lord, they are actually completely free from material attachments.

Renunciants are supposed to surrender their lives completely to the service of the Lord. Usually, renunciants perform all their responsibilities to serve the Lord, depending wholeheartedly on the Lord's mercy. We know how the Six Goswamis, Chaitanya Mahaprabhu, and many other spiritual preceptors in our line begged alms in order to serve the Lord. They didn't beg in order to fill their bellies; rather, their practice of begging (*madhukari*) was aimed at destroying their egos, which were born of high birth, wealth, education, and beauty. However, in the present age of hypocrisy, Kali-yuga, we see that most renunciants, in the name of serving the Lord, establish large temples and organizations to provide for their personal maintenance. To sustain these organizations they have different types of hospitality businesses rather than depending on the Lord's mercy. Outwardly, it looks like these renunciants are doing everything for the Lord, but the duties of the renounced ashram don't include engaging in business. In reality, these renunciants are establishing temples and organizations as a way to garner material name, fame, and recognition that will guarantee their futures. When such so-called renounced persons dress like monks and engage in these business activities, we can't call them *anasakta*, "materially detached." Bhaktivinode Thakur writes that true renunciants are rarely found in this age. In the *Bhaktivinoda Vani Vaibhava* we find this statement: "When we see many monks in society wearing red or saffron cloth, we must most certainly understand that something is not right in society."

At the same time, if householders wishing to serve the Lord use these same types of businesses to maintain their families, they can be considered *anasakta*. This is because the ashram dharma of renounced persons (*brahmacharis*, *vanaprasthas*, and *sannyasis*) doesn't allow for any activity aimed at financial sustainability. If we look closer, we'll see that renounced persons who do business to maintain themselves have lost faith that the Lord is their only maintainer and protector. Instead, they have developed faith in business schemes. In *Sharanagati* Bhaktivinode Thakur writes, *avashya rakshibe krishna vishvasa palana*: "Krishna is our sole protector." We must believe this from the bottom of our hearts.

The words *samsara tathaya paya parabhava* help us understand that we're eligible to cross the ocean of material birth and death when we maintain the principles of the ashram in which we are situated (*brahmacharya*, *grihasthya*, *vanaprastha*, or *sannyasa*) without material attachment. Also, we must simultaneously render service to Krishna and His pure devotees. There should be a balance between maintaining ashram duties and serving Krishna. The goal of maintaining one's ashram and *varna* is to serve Krishna.

> *cāri-varṇāśrami yadi kṛṣṇa nāhi bhaje*
> *sva-karma karile-o raurave paḍi maje*

"If people situated in their respective *varna* and ashram are not serving Krishna but simply performing material duties, they will fall into a hellish condition." However, it's important to note that this doesn't mean, in the name of serving Krishna, that we should give up our duties according to *varnashrama*.

We can cure physical diseases with medical assistance. The words *yathayogya-bhoga* in Srila Prabhupada's verse mean we should serve the Lord while fulfilling our material duties. Attention to material duties in this context doesn't mean we have the disease of material attachment. There is nothing more to be said on this topic of material detachment. It's not a question of external show; rather, our success depends on our sincerity.

Text 12

'āsakti-rahita' 'sambandha-sahita'
viṣayasamūha sakali 'mādhava'
se 'yuktavairagya', tāhā ta' saubhāgya',
tāhāi jaḍete harira vaibhava

Word-for-word

āsakti – material attachment; *rahita* – free from; *sambandha* – relation; *sahita* – with; *viṣayasamūha* – material sense objects; *sakali* – all; *mādhava* – another name of Lord Krishna; *se* – that; *yuktavairagya* – renunciation for the pleasure of the Lord according to time, place, and circumstance; *tāhā* – that; *ta'* – is; *saubhāgya* – fortune; *tāhāi* – that is; *jaḍete* – in the material world; *harira* – Hari's; *vaibhava* – glory.

Translation

Being free of material attachment, knowing that everything is related to Madhava and to be used in His service, is called *yukta-vairagya,* or renunciation appropriate for giving the Lord pleasure. Those who practice *yukta-vairagya* are fortunate. That, in and of itself, is the glory of Lord Hari in the material world.

Commentary

Krishna owns the entire universe. Due to the influence of the material, illusory energy, we think the world is our property. This understanding is called *asakti,* or material attachment. It's our goal in spiritual practice to become free from *asakti.* We may pretend that we're free of material attachment, but it's difficult to be totally free unless we get the Lord's blessings. When we're free of material attachment we understand the essence of the material world. This mortal world is unstable; it changes at every moment. Our body is material. Therefore, we can see our body is changing all the time. For instance, if a man compares photos of himself at two years old and at thirty years old, he may not even recognize that both photos are of himself, especially if he hasn't ever seen a photo of himself at two.

The mind also changes constantly. One day

we think someone a friend and the next day an enemy. Even property – one day some property belongs to us, and some days later, that property may be owned by someone else. It's strange that we remain attached to such transient material wealth. Everything material changes constantly, but it's unfortunate that our minds, hearts, intelligence, and consciousness remain attached to this temporary, changing matter. When we're able to fix the mind, heart, intelligence, and consciousness on the Lord and His service, without mundane expectations, then we are considered free of material attachment (*asakti-rahita*) and properly established in our relationship as servants of the Lord (*sambandha-sahita*). If we have mundane expectations, then even if we fix the mind on the Supreme Lord, we cannot be considered free from material attachment or properly connected with the Lord.

Day after day we face so many troubles, so many problems to solve, in order to survive in the material world. These problems come in the form of the threefold miseries of material existence, namely miseries coming from the body and mind (*adhyatmika*), from other living entities (*adhibhautika*), and from nature (weather and natural disasters), caused by the higher living entities (*adhidaivika*). The material world is like an ocean; the problems are the ocean's waves. We think we'll bathe in the ocean when the waves stop, but we can be certain that we will never be able to bathe there. Similarly, if we think we'll render service to the Lord once our material problems are solved, we can be sure that we will never serve the Lord.

Our previous teachers therefore used a significant word: *yukta-vairagya*. There will always be problems in this world, but the Lord's service has to go on. For example, winter is a problem because it is cold. Rain is also an inconvenience because we get wet. Both of these appear to be impediments, but in the spirit of *yukta-vairagya*, or using everything in the Lord's service according to time, place, and circumstance, we can be intelligent and protect ourselves. When it's cold we can wear warm clothes, and when it rains we can carry an umbrella. As long as our aim is to serve the Lord with no tinge of selfishness and without expecting anything in return, then we can use anything in the spirit of *yukta-vairagya*. Whenever we practice *yukta-vairagya* we realize our great fortune in being able to establish our eternal identity in such a manner, despite any obstacles. The

Supreme Lord is happy to see our endeavors in His service.

When we first came to our temple in Mayapur, there was no running water, no proper kitchen, no comfortable toilets or bathrooms, and no bedrooms for the devotees. There was one room for the deities and one for *gurudeva*. There was not enough money for our daily service expenses. We used to live on the open veranda in any weather. Despite all these obstacles, we applied our intelligence according to time, place, and circumstance to enthusiastically serve Lord Hari. We know that Lord Hari's happiness is His devotees' happiness. By practicing *yukta-vairagya* we found that both the devotees and the Lord were blissful. This is the glory of the Lord and His devotees.

Srila Prabhupada Bhaktisiddhanta Saraswati Goswami Thakur wanted to teach us that despite all obstacles we should apply our intelligence to serve the Lord constantly according to time, place, and circumstance, without complaint and without mundane expectations. As we are followers of Prabhupada Bhaktisiddhanta and his disciples, we should always keep in mind how our previous teachers laid the path and gave us methods to navigate past all obstacles through *yukta-vairagya.* Practicing *yukta-vairagya* allows us to gradually establish our eternal identity as the Supreme Lord's eternal servants. We shall eternally serve the Divine Couple and Their devotees under the guidance of our previous teachers.

Text 13

kīrtane yāhāra, 'pratiṣṭhā-sambhāra'
tāhāra sampatti kevala 'kaitava'
'viṣaya-mumukṣu' 'bhogera bubhukṣu'
duye tyaja mana, dui – 'avaiṣṇava'

Word-for-word

kīrtane – by congregationally chanting the holy names; *yāhāra* – whose; *pratiṣṭhā-sambhāra* – aim is just to garner material name, fame, and recognition; *tāhāra* – such a person's; *sampatti* – livelihood; *kevala* – only; *kaitava* – hypocrisy; *viṣaya-mumukṣu* – desiring freedom from material sense enjoyment; *bhogera-bubhuksu* – desiring to enjoy material sense enjoyment; *duye* – both; *tyaja* – give up; *mana* – mind; *dui* – both; *avaiṣṇava* – are qualities which do not befit a pure devotee.

Translation

Whoever glorifies the Lord for material name and fame and makes a livelihood out of that is engaged only in hypocrisy. O mind, give up both the desire for material sense enjoyment and the desire to be free of material sense enjoyment. These two desires do not befit pure devotees – they are *avaishnava*.

Commentary

In this day and age, when most people glorify the Lord it is to gain recognition from their audience. Thus we can see that many people give *Srimad-Bhagavatam* discourses accompanied by musical instruments and melodious singers. Such speakers claim that if someone listens to their discourses for seven days, he or she will be delivered from the material universe. They give the example of Dundukari and Gokarna, a story sometimes told to glorify the power of *Srimad-Bhagavatam*. Here is the story.

There once was a *brahmana* named Atmadeva, who was married to Dhunduli. They had no children even after years of marriage. Not only that, but none of their cows could get pregnant, and even the fruit trees in their garden produced no fruit. At that time people had a superstition that if a couple remained childless they were inauspicious for the whole society. Therefore the neighbors refused to even see the faces of Atmadeva and his wife, believing that if they saw their faces they would themselves not get the fruits of whatever work they had performed that day.

Atmadeva was discouraged by his neighbors' behavior and thought of committing suicide. One day he left home and wandered deep into the forest. Thirsty, he saw a lake and decided to drink. While he was by that lake he found a renunciant. The monk asked him why he was depressed. Atmadeva explained his situation, and somehow the monk was able to predict his future: "For the next seven lives you will have no children."

However, Atmadeva repeatedly asked the *sannyasi* to bless him with a child. Gravely, the *sannyasi* said, "Don't go against the will of the Lord. Maharaj Chitraketu had one hundred thousand wives, but no children. In order to change his destiny he asked Angira Rishi to perform a fire sacrifice. A fruit came from that sacrifice, and Angira Rishi instructed Chitraketu to give it to his favorite wife. When the baby was born, Chitraketu was happy, but his other wives were extremely jealous and concluded that their unhappiness had been caused by the baby. They conspired to kill the prince. After the prince died, Chitraketu Maharaj was even more depressed."

The *sannyasi* continued, "Atmadeva, you should accept whatever the Lord has written for you in your destiny. Don't try to go against His will."

But Atmadeva refused this advice. Instead, he nagged the *sannyasi* for the blessing of a child. Finally, the *sannyasi* gave Atmadeva a piece of fruit, instructing him to feed it to Dhunduli. For one year, the *sannyasi* said, she should follow a vow of eating only once a day, and she should always be truthful, pure, kind, and charitable. After that year she would become pregnant. Atmadeva quickly brought the fruit home and gave it to his wife, describing everything that had happened.

Dhunduli revealed everything to her friend, including her concerns about becoming pregnant. "If I only eat once a day, as the monk requested, I will not have the strength to do my household duties and won't be able to bear the pain of childbirth." Her friend agreed with Dhunduli out of respect.

Then, a few days later, Dhunduli's sister visited. Again Dhunduli related the whole story. On hearing of Dhunduli's situation, the sister, who was pregnant at the time, suggested that she give Dhunduli her baby, and that Dhunduli should pretend to be pregnant. She also asked Dhunduli to give the fruit to one of the cows in the *goshala*.

When the sister's baby was born, he was given to Dhunduli as promised, and Atmadeva, not knowing what the two women had done, named him Dhundukari. Both Atmadeva and his neighbors were happy to be blessed by a newborn. But since Dhunduli had not actually been pregnant she had no breast milk with which to feed the baby. She presented the situation to her husband. "We have a problem. I don't have any breast milk, but there is a solution. My sister also gave birth to a baby, but by some misfortune her baby died. So if you don't mind, I will ask my sister to stay in our house, and in this way, she can breastfeed our baby." Atmadeva agreed to Dhunduli's proposal.

Three months later, the cow that had eaten the *sannyasi*'s fruit gave birth to a human baby, surprising everyone. No one knew, of course, what had really transpired. Since this baby was born from a cow and had the ears of a cow, the neighbors named him Gokarna (*go* means "cow" and *karna* means "ears"). Atmadeva and his neighbors became overjoyed to see both children.

When Dhundukari began to grow up, he began to steal and was always angry. He didn't like people, and he hurt children by throwing them into a well. He also kept the association of prostitutes. Dhundukari got worse as the days passed, so much so that he created chaos at home, draining his family's finances in order to satisfy his addiction to prostitutes. Gokarna, however, was the opposite. He was quiet, calm, and fully absorbed in spiritual practice.

Seeing his first son's condition, Atmadeva felt dejected and again thought of committing suicide by drowning, entering fire, or throwing himself off a cliff. Observing his father's lamentation, however, Gokarna encouraged Atmadeva to give up his attachment to wife, sons, and wealth and to adopt a life of renunciation. Atmadeva asked what he would do in the forest, and Gokarna replied, "You should give up your identification with your temporary material body and spend the rest of your life hearing about the transcendental pastimes of Lord Vishnu." On hearing his son's instruction, Atmadeva left home and found association amid Lord Vishnu's devotees. He eventually attained the Lord's transcendental abode.

After Atmadeva left, Dhundukari asked his

mother for more money, threatening to kill her if she didn't comply. Afraid, that night she too left home. In the dark she fell into a well, where she was welcomed by death. After this incident, Gokarna went on pilgrimage, visiting various holy places, and Dhundukari stayed home and continued with his immoral behavior of maintaining prostitutes, moving them into his own house.

But after some time the prostitutes became restless. They demanded clothes and jewelry from Dhundukari, which he could not afford, and so they threatened to leave him. Afraid of losing their company, Dhundukari stole clothes and jewelry from other people's houses and gave them to his kept women. Understanding how Dhundukari had acquired these items, the prostitutes thought, "The king will surely arrest him and strip us of all these goods. Better that we kill him and leave this place." So that night, while he was sleeping, they tried to strangle him, but he didn't die. Then they resorted to burning his face with hot coals. This eventually killed him, and they disposed of his body and left.

After his pilgrimage, Gokarna returned to his village. One night, the fearful ghost of Dhundukari arrived in a terrible form. Dhundukari had developed the ability to shapeshift, and doing this he was able to awaken Gokarna. On seeing this, fierce form, Gokarna asked, "Who are you and why are you trying to frighten me? Why are you such in a pitiable condition? Can I help you?"

Dhundukari wept to hear these kind words, but he was unable to answer because he was so thirsty. Seeing that the ghost was indicating thirst, Gokarna took water from his water pot and threw it on the ghost. The creature then began to speak. "O my brother, Gokarna, please help me." Dhundukari told Gokarna his story and repeatedly asked Gokarna to deliver him from his hell.

Gokarna told Dhundukari that he had performed a *shraddha* ceremony both for him and their departed father in Gaya. Why, Gokarna wondered, had his brother not been delivered by this rite? The next morning he went to see a learned *brahmana* to ask about this. The *brahmana* prayed to Suryadeva, the sun god, who said, "The only way Dhundukari can be delivered is by hearing *Srimad-Bhagavatam* recited for seven consecutive days."

Gokarna then went to the banks of the Tungabhadra River and began to recite the *Bhagavatam* in the association of many sages. Dhundukari also came to hear, entering a bamboo stalk that had seven knots. He remained for all seven days, and at the end of each day's listening, one of the bamboo's knots would open with a loud *crack*! At the end of the seventh day, the bamboo stalk toppled over and a flower chariot descended from the spiritual abode. Gokarna saw his brother climb onto the chariot and return to Vaikuntha.

So nowadays, most *Bhagavatam* speakers advertise that people who listen to their talks for seven days, like Dhundukari, will be delivered. But Gokarna never brought teams of singers or musicians to his *Bhagavatam* recitations – nothing to distract his listeners. These days, most speakers want to become famous, so they use dramatic rhetoric and enchanting music to attract the audience. Such methods used to please the audience do not please the Lord. Moreover, since the speaker is motivated by his own material interest, and the listeners by their desire to be entertained by melodious music and dramatic explanations, neither the speaker nor their thousands of listeners have any chance to receive spiritual benefit, not to speak of deliverance from the material world.

In this regard, I would like to describe another incident, this one involving one of our great teachers, His Divine Grace Srila Gaura Kishor Das Babaji Maharaj. Babaji Maharaj was famous throughout Navadvipa and Vrindavan as a pure devotee. There was a business-minded *Bhagavatam* speaker in the Navadvipa area who used to give discourses in exchange for money. One day, the *Bhagavatam* speaker thought that if he gave a discourse in Babaji Maharaj's presence he could raise his fees. So Babaji Maharaj was brought to the *Bhagavatam* program. Babaji Maharaj attended all seven days. At the end of the week the speaker took his entire audience and went to speak to Babaji Maharaj, asking him how he'd liked the discourse. Babaji Maharaj replied, "*Bhagavatam*? Where? There were no *Bhagavatam* discourses here. I heard only 'Money, money, money.' There was no glorification of the *Bhagavatam*. I feel that one foot of soil should be dug up and removed from the place where you sat and spoke, as it has become impure."

Here in this verse, His Divine Grace Srila Prabhupada Bhaktisiddhanta Saraswati Thakur is trying to help us understand that the goal of giving discourses should be to purify ourselves and please the Lord with our devotional mood. However, these days we have lost sight of our devotion and are simply trying to please the audience and garner recognition – material name and fame – and make more money. Although we may attend artistic and dramatic explanations of *Srimad-Bhagavatam,* we should understand that these are all hypocrisy. The speakers and listeners are both being cheated. This is a prime example of hypocrisy in today's spiritual organizations.

In the name of practicing spirituality, some people present themselves as extremely renounced. Others present themselves as extremely opulent. Both are using their respective presentations to gain recognition for themselves. In this verse, *vishayera-mumukshu* refers to those who want to be free of material sense enjoyment in their presentation of spiritual practice, and *bhogera-bubhukshu* refers to those who want lots of material sense enjoyment in order to show their spiritual advancement. People in this second category, in the name of attracting large numbers of people to practice spirituality, may construct temples that are more opulent than those established by our previous teachers. Others make a show of extreme poverty to make people think that they are highly elevated, fully detached, and renounced. Sometimes they even go so far as to reject donations, making themselves look disinterested in material wealth. Neither of these tendencies are supported by the teachings of our spiritual lineage.

Rather, the main goal of our practice is to please the Lord without expectation of anything in return. Whenever we have material expectations – desires for name, fame, recognition, money, power, or position – the actions we perform become karma instead of *bhakti*. *Bhakti* means "honest love for Krishna." Honest love means we're prepared to give everything to please the object of our love, without selfish expectations. The teachers in our lineage have instructed us that our goal is to become neither enjoyers nor renunciants. Neither of these two are pure devotees. O mind! Give up both tendencies. Try to wholeheartedly serve the object of your love, the Divine Couple, Sri Sri Radha Govinda.

Text 14

'kṛṣṇera sambandha', aprākṛta-skandha,
kabhu nahe tāhā jaḍera sambhava
'māyāvādī jana' kṛṣṇetara mana,
mukta abhimāne se ninde vaiṣṇava

Word-for-word

kṛṣṇera – Krishna's; *sambandha* – relationship; *aprākṛta* – spiritual; *skandha* – shelter; *kabhu nahe* – never; *tāhā* – that; *jaḍera sambhava* – possibility of being material; *māyāvādī* – those who desire to merge into the formless effulgence of the Lord; *jana* – people; *kṛṣṇetara mana* – minds engaged in topics that are inferior to topics about Krishna; *mukta* – liberated; *abhimāne* – in pride; *se* – such a person; *ninde* – criticizes; *vaiṣṇava* – the pure devotees.

Translation

Those who have established a relationship with Krishna are always under the shelter of the transcendental energy; there is no tinge of material connection in their relationship with Krishna. Those who imagine themselves to be God, desiring to merge into the formless effulgence of Lord Vishnu [Mayavadis], think themselves liberated from the material energy. In their pride they always think negatively about Lord Krishna, so they criticize the Lord and His devotees [Vaishnavas].

Commentary

As soon as we're able to establish our eternal relationship with Lord Krishna, we immediately come under the shelter of the Lord's transcendental energy. In this context I would like to describe an incident between Lala Babu and Jagat Shetha.

Both Lala Babu and Jagat Shetha were wealthy; they were also competitors. Lala Babu was a rich landlord who collected taxes from his residents. Both of them eventually lived in Vrindavan. Jagat Shetha retired to Vrindavan with his family first, while Lala remained absorbed in his work. Lala Babu arrived in Vrindavan later. His inspiration to retire came one day when he was being carried on a palanquin near a lake. A washerman and his family were preparing to wash clothes. It was almost noon. As he passed he heard the washerman's daughter ask her father, "Time has passed since we came out. When will you kindle the fire so we can heat the water for the laundry?"

Lala Babu suddenly thought, "Yes, much time has passed. My life is almost over! What have I done with my life? I should immediately leave all this material work behind and go to Vrindavan, accept a guru, and begin my spiritual practice."

Lala Babu then left for Vrindavan and met an elevated guru, who was in the renounced order. Lala Babu asked him for initiation, but the guru said, "You are not ready. You still have a lot of ego, so you are not qualified to be initiated by me. First remove all your ego. Then you will become qualified for initiation."

To destroy his ego, Lala Babu decided to live by begging alms instead of relying on the money he had previously saved. After several months of begging, he again approached the guru, but the guru again told him he had too much ego. Lala Babu became introspective. "What ego remains?"

He realized, "I still have one type of ego left. I didn't go to Jagat Shetha to beg alms from him during all these months."

So the next day Lala Babu went to Jagat Shetha's house to beg alms. Jagat Shetha was happy to see that Lala Babu had humbled himself. Lala Babu and Jagat Shetha had once been intensely competitive, but now they hugged each other. After this, Lala Babu again approached the guru, and this time the guru told him he was qualified for initiation.

This incident teaches us that when we want to realize our eternal identity as the eternal servant of the Lord, we must first become completely free from material attachment, ego, pride, and the desire for material name, fame, and recognition. When we're attached to false prestige, it isn't possible to establish our relationship with Krishna. Thus we see in this story that the guru, who is Krishna's representative, initially refused to initiate Lala Babu because he was maintaining his competitive spirit with Jagat Shetha. When Lala Babu realized that his competitive relationship with Jagat Shetha was due to his *own* competitive nature, he went to beg alms from Jagat Shetha. This allowed the last remnants of ego to be destroyed. The guru then agreed to initiate Lala Babu and connect him with Lord Krishna. Initiation means to become connected with Lord Krishna through the transparent via medium of the guru. Although the disciple sees the guru as nondifferent from Krishna, the guru thinks of himself as being the servant of the servant of the servant of Krishna.

Mayavadis are defined as those who want to merge into the formless effulgence of the Lord. They believe that the Supreme Lord has no eternal name, form, or qualities. They act like they believe in the Lord, but really, they are atheists. They try to attain their chosen destination by depending solely on their own study and practice (*arohavadi*). Moreover, Mayavadis are totally opposed to the idea of surrendering to the Supreme Lord and His pure devotees.

On the other hand, the Lord's pure devotees understand that the Supreme Lord possesses an eternal name, form, qualities, and pastimes. They are straightforward and genuinely theistic, and they try to attain their chosen destination by depending on the mercy of their spiritual teachers, other pure devotees, and the Lord, as well as their spiritual practice (*avarohavadi*). Vaishnavas engage in one-pointed surrender to the Lord and His pure devotees.

Mayavadis are opportunistic. For example, a man climbs a tall tree by using a ladder, stepping up rung by rung until he successfully reaches the treetop. Once he has achieved his goal, however, he kicks the ladder away. He doesn't become thankful for the assistance he was given, nor does he give credit to the ladder. We see that same ingratitude in Mayavadis. Mayavadis think themselves to be God and so want to merge into the formless effulgence rather than accept an eternal identity as God's servants. Their misconception is based on wanting to remain a controller and to lord over everything they see. Nowadays, most Mayavadi spiritual leaders misuse the concept of guru as it is described in the sacred scriptures. We know from *shastra* that guru and Krishna are nondifferent. The Mayavadis take advantage of this and act as if they themselves are God. They portray themselves as more merciful than Krishna. As a result, these days we see a number of Mayavadi gurus going to jail, accused of murder, rape, money-laundering, and other crimes. They become entangled in all these activities due to ego, pride, and living in the mode of passion.

By contrast, Krishna's devotees voluntarily

accept their eternal identity as eternal servants of the servants of the servants of Krishna. We know that Krishna in the form of Sri Krishna Chaitanya Mahaprabhu taught:

nāhaṁ vipro na ca nara-patir nāpi vaiśyo na
śūdro
nāhaṁ varṇī na ca gṛha-patir no vanastho
yatir vā
kintu prodyan-nikhila-paramananda-
purṇāmṛtābdher
gopī-bhartuḥ pada-kamalayor dāsa-
dāsānudāsaḥ

"I am not a *brahmana* [topmost caste, head of society], *kshatriya* [soldier, king, or other government administrator], *vaishya* [businessman or farmer], or *shudra* [one who works for the other three castes]. I am not a *brahmachari* [celibate student], *grihastha* [householder], *vanaprastha* [retired spiritual practitioner], or *sannyasi* [mendicant]. I am the eternal servant of the servant of the servant of the maintainer of the *gopis,* who are the intimate servants of Lord Krishna in Vrindavan. That Vrindavan Krishna who is brilliant and a complete ocean of universal nectarine bliss."

From this verse we understand that no one can ever be superior to Krishna, not to speak of equal to Him. Everyone is lower than Krishna. Thus the pure devotees, from the cores of their hearts, joyfully accept their position as eternal servants of the servants of the servants of the Supreme Lord, Sri Krishna.

Vaishnavas never criticize anyone. They are fully surrendered to Him and His pure devotees. By nature they are humbler than a blade of grass and more tolerant than a tree. They are completely free from false prestige and the desire for material name, fame, recognition, worship, and so on. They respect everyone and do not expect respect from anyone.

However, Mayavadis think themselves liberated and imagine themselves to be God. Thus in their pride they criticize the Vaishnavas. Mayavadis think Vaishnavas inferior to themselves because Vaishnavas prefer to serve Krishna rather than to be God.

Text 15

vaiṣṇavera dāsa, tava-bhakti-āśa,
kena vā ḍākicha nirjana-āhaba
ye 'phalgu vairāgī', kahe, nije, 'tyāgī',
se nā pāre kabhu haite 'vaiṣṇava'

Word-for-word

vaiṣṇavera – of the pure devotees; *dāsa* – servant; *tava* – your; *bhakti* – devotion; *āśa* – hope; *kena vā* – why are you; *ḍākicha* – praying; *nirjana* – in solitude; *āhaba* – calling out; *ye* – that; *phalgu* – fake; *vairāgī* – renounced person; *kahe* – says; *nije* – to himself; *tyāgī* – renunciant; *se* – that; *nā* – not; *pāre* – can; *kabhu* – ever; *haite* – to be; *vaiṣṇava* – pure devotee

Translation

O mind! Your only hope on the path of devotion is to serve pure devotees. Why are you praying and calling out to the Lord from your solitary place? False renunciants consider themselves *tyagis*. Such hypocrites can never become pure devotees.

Commentary

It's impossible for us in our conditioned state to get Krishna's mercy directly – that is, by sitting in a solitary place and chanting. We are filled with too many unwanted material desires (*anarthas*), and this makes us ineligible to attain the Supreme Lord's mercy directly. It's true that the Supreme Lord is always trying to bestow His mercy on us, though, and so He sends us His blessings through His pure devotees. When we're able to please a pure devotee by our service attitude, then we can receive the Supreme Lord's mercy as it flows through that pure devotee.

To illustrate this I would like to offer a glimpse into Narottama Das Thakur's life. Before Narottama was born, Chaitanya Mahaprabhu visited Kheturi, a village on the bank of the Padma River, on His way to Vrindavan. There He chanted, "Naru! Naru!" No one could understand what He was saying or why. It's said that Mahaprabhu stored divine love (*prema*) in the Padma River as He called out "Naru! Naru!"

Several years later, "Naru," Narottama Das Thakur, appeared in Kheturi. Narottama Das Thakur was not an ordinary boy but the prince of Kheturi. In his eternal position he is Champaka Manjari.

When Narottama Das Thakur was twelve, Chaitanya Mahaprabhu appeared to him in a dream and instructed him to accept initiation from Lokanath Goswami. Narottama immediately set out for Vrindavan, although the path to Vrindavan at that time was very difficult. He went barefoot. On the way, Narottama constantly heard Krishna's flute-song, and he followed that melody toward Vrindavan. This is how Krishna guided him on his journey.

On the way, Narottama Thakur met Jahnava Mata, Nityananda Prabhu's internal potency. In the spiritual abode, Jahnava Mata is Ananga Manjari. Narottama Das Thakur received her mercy.

When he finally arrived in Vrindavan and met Lokanath Goswami, the *sadhu* was astonished to hear Narottama's proposal that Lokanath initiate him. Lokanath Goswami said, "I have vowed not to initiate anyone. Better to find someone else from whom you can take initiation."

Narottama Thakur was confused by this response. He wanted to serve Lokanath Goswami, but Lokanath Goswami did not allow anyone to serve him. Actually, this is the natural feeling of a pure devotee – pure devotees are extremely humble and feel themselves ineligible to be served by anyone. But if we don't serve a pure devotee of the Lord, we will be unable to receive the Lord's blessings.

Narottama Das Thakur was eventually inspired to serve Lokanath Goswami secretly by cleaning the place where Lokanath Goswami went for his ablutions. So every day, Narottama Das Thakur placed a clean neem twig, clay, and water for Lokanath Goswami's use. In those days, people brushed their teeth with neem twigs and washed their hands with clay instead of soap. After several days, Lokanath Goswami realized someone was making these preparations for him. "Who is doing this?" he wondered. "I have to know."

So one day, Lokanath Goswami decided to go to that place early, just to see who was performing such menial service. There he found Prince Narottama cleaning the place. Lokanath Goswami was surprised and said, "O Narottama, you are a prince, yet you are doing such menial service. I must now break my vow." Narottama Das Thakur's eyes filled with tears of bliss. Lokanath Goswami said, "Go and bathe in the river and then come to me. I will initiate you today."

Therefore, in Prabhupada's verse he tells us we must serve pure Vaishnavas and surrender to them – such service and surrender is the life and soul of pure devotional practice. If instead we choose to sit in a solitary place, chanting the Hare Krishna *maha-mantra,* we will never get the chance to truly surrender to the Lord and His devotees. Without surrender, the life and soul of devotion, we will never receive the blessings necessary to progress on our devotional path.

In this regard I would like to tell the story of Shabari and Matanga Rishi, who lived during Lord Ramachandra's time. Shabari had a strong desire to spend her life serving pure devotees. At that time, as was the tradition, her parents arranged her wedding before Shabari became a teenager. Shabari realized that if she got married she wouldn't be able to fulfill her inner desire to dedicate her life to the service of the Lord's pure devotees. So on her wedding day she ran away from home. Walking a long distance, she eventually reached Kishkindha, on the bank of a lake called Pampa. Hanuman, the son of Anjana Devi, was born at Kishkindha, and there she saw many renounced mendicants living in small cottages. Renounced mendicants traditionally do not accept service from anyone, not to speak of from young girls. So Shabari chose to do her service secretly. While the renounced mendicants slept she entered the ashram area and cleaned and swept it. Seeing that the mendicants had to go deep into the jungle to collect firewood, she herself went into the jungle, piling whatever wood she collected near the *sadhus'* cottages. She felt that it was better for her to go into the jungle than the mendicants. The firewood she brought to their homes was easily accessed for their fire sacrifices and cooking.

Several months passed in this way, with Shabari continuing to secretly render her service. Then one day, Matanga Rishi happened to see that Shabari was doing these services. Although Matanga Rishi had vowed to never initiate a woman, on discovering Shabari's exemplary service, performed without desire for recognition, he broke his vow and initiated her. Afterward, he told her, "Soon, Lord Rama will come to this area. Please prepare yourself to greet Him to the best of your ability."

From that day forward, Shabari picked flowers every day and decorated the path to her ashram as she waited for Lord Rama's arrival. She also picked fruits and kept them ready for Him. But many years passed and Lord Rama did not come. Matanga Rishi left this world and Shabari grew very old. She could no longer see properly. Still, despite her age, she daily followed her guru's order and prepared to receive Lord Rama.

Suddenly, one day Rama and Lakshman (who were Krishna and Balaram in Dvapara-yuga and Chaitanya and Nityananda in Kali-yuga) appeared at Shabari's cottage. Like every other day she had already prepared to receive Them with the flower path and the fresh fruit. She had Rama and Lakshman sit down, and she fed Lord Ramachandra the forest berries she had picked. Berries are sometimes sweet and sometimes sour. She wanted to offer Lord Rama only the sweet ones, so she bit each berry to see whether or not it was sweet, discarding the sour ones. Each sweet berry she tasted she offered to Lord Rama, who ate her offerings happily. Lakshman, however, tried to stop Him. How could He accept berries that had already been tasted? But Lord Rama replied, "Although they are Shabari's remnants, these berries are extremely sweet and filled with love."

Here again we see that unless we serve and please the pure devotees, we will be ineligible to connect with the Lord, serve Him, and receive His mercy. Serving pure devotees does not only mean serving them physically; we should also wholeheartedly follow their instructions. Following the instructions of pure devotees is also considered serving them. As already stated, surrender is the life and soul of devotional practice. Only by devotion can we reach the Lord and experience His supreme sweetness. Therefore, Prabhupada says that one who calls himself a *tyagi* – a solitary practitioner – and who chants the Lord's names in private is actually a false renunciant. False renunciants are unable to become pure devotees. We become purified only when we get the blessings of pure devotees, and those blessings come only when we serve those devotees.

It is well known that human culture, attitudes,

food habits, and so on, are dictated by others. Cultures, attitudes, and habits are not God-given but are learned through association. Serving pure devotees teaches us a culture and attitudes that are purifying. His Divine Grace Srila Prabhupada Bhaktisiddhanta Saraswati Thakur is therefore here inspiring us to remain in the association of like-minded devotees who are more elevated than ourselves and to serve them in a devotional mood. In this way, we can practice the path of pure devotion, which is the only way we can be delivered from material existence, realize our eternal identities, and reach the eternal abode of the Divine Couple, Sri Sri Radha and Krishna, the topmost goal of our human lives. Again, all of this is possible only if we serve pure devotees.

Text 16

haripada chāḍi', 'nirjanatā bāḍi'
labhiyā ki phala, 'phalgu' se vaibhava
rādhādāsye rahi' chāḍa 'bhoga-ahi'
'pratiṣṭhāśā' nahe 'kīrtana-gaurava'

Word-for-word

haripada – the lotus feet of Lord Hari; *chāḍi'* – giving up; *nirjanatā* – solitary *bāḍi* – home; *labhiyā* – gaining; *ki* – what; *phala* – useless; *phalgu* – false; *se* – that; *vaibhava* – opulence; *rādhādāsye* – in the service of Radharani; *rahi'* – being situated; *chāḍa* – give up; *bhoga-ahi* – the indulgence of sitting in solitude and making a show of chanting; *pratiṣṭhāśā* – desire for gaining material name, fame, and worship; *nahe* – is never; *kīrtana-gaurava* – glorification of the Lord's divine names.

Translation

What is the use of making a show of chanting the holy names, sitting in a solitary place, and renouncing our service to the lotus feet of Lord Hari and His pure devotees? The opulence and material recognition you gain from the public through your show of solitary chanting is useless. Situate yourself in your eternal position as the maidservant of Srimati Radharani. Give up your solitary indulgence. Your desire to gain material name, fame, and recognition is not genuine glorification of Lord Hari's names.

Commentary

A few days before his physical departure, His Divine Grace Srila Prabhupada Bhaktisiddhanta Saraswati Thakur said that everyone should unite under one shelter: Srimati Radharani. This is because Srimati Radharani is our *acharya*. The actual *acharya* teaches aspiring devotees the topmost method of service to the Supreme Lord. No one can render service equal to the service offered by Radharani, not to speak of surpassing Her. Prabhupada instructed his followers to spread the loving message of Rupa Goswami and Raghunath Das Goswami with supreme enthusiasm. Chanting the holy names gives us the qualification to serve the Lord. If we chant the holy names alone with a desire to gain material name and fame, then it is understood that this is not true glorification of Lord Hari. Such a show is useless (*phalgu*). However, if we chant the holy names alone with the blessings of the *guru-parampara* and a desire to become spiritually strong enough to spread the message of Rupa and Raghunath, then that's understood to be genuine glorification of Lord Hari.

Before spreading the loving message of Lord Chaitanya, His Divine Grace Srila Prabhupada Bhaktisiddhanta Saraswati Thakur sat in a solitary place in Mayapur with a vow to chant one billion holy names. Completing such a vow would take more than ten years for someone chanting three hundred thousand names (192 rounds) per day. We shouldn't think that Prabhupada was sitting alone and chanting in order to indulge a desire for material recognition. Rather, his solitary practice was performed to fulfill the will of Lord Chaitanya: *prthivite ache yata nagaradi-grama sarvatra prachara haibe mora nama* – "My holy names will be spread in every town and village on the earth." After completing his vow, Prabhupada Bhaktisiddhanta Saraswati Thakur started to preach, first alone, and then later by sending his disciples to various places all over the world.

We know that in 1930, Prabhupada sent three of his disciples, namely His Divine Grace Bhakti Pradipa Tirtha Goswami Maharaj, His Divine Grace Bhakti Hridaya Vana Goswami Maharaj, and His Divine Grace Bhakti Saranga Goswami Maharaj, abroad to preach the message of Lord Chaitanya. Prabhupada Bhaktisiddhanta also instructed one of his householder disciples, Abhaya Charanaravinda Das Adhikari, to preach in the Western countries, since this disciple was proficient in English. In 1959, Abhaya Charanaravinda Das Adhikari took *sannyasa* from his senior godbrother, His Divine Grace Bhakti Prajnan Keshav Goswami Maharaj, who was the founder of the Gaudiya Vedanta Samiti. Abhaya Charanaravinda Das Adhikari received the name His Divine Grace Bhaktivedanta Swami Maharaj. Before fulfilling the desire of his *gurudeva,* Prabhupada Bhaktisiddhanta Saraswati Thakur, that he spread the loving message of Lord Chaitanya in the Western world, he spent his valuable time from 1950 to 1965 alone at the Radha-Damodar Mandir in Vrindavan, chanting the holy names and translating the *Bhagavat Purana* into English.

With the blessings of his *gurudeva* he went to the Western world in 1965 and massively spread the loving message of Lord Chaitanya all over the world. Nowadays, he is famously known as His Divine Grace A. C. Bhaktivedanta Swami Prabhupada, founder of the International Society for Krishna Consciousness (ISKCON).

His Divine Grace Bhakti Dayita Madhava Goswami Maharaj, founder of Sri Chaitanya Gaudiya Math, spread the loving message of Lord Chaitanya all over India in order to fulfill the desire of his *gurudeva*, Prabhupada Bhaktisiddhanta Saraswati Thakur. He especially preached in areas where the Mayavadi philosophy was rampant, and he helped many Mayavadis to transform into servants of Lord Chaitanya's loving mission. He wholeheartedly served all his godbrothers and other Vaishnavas. Through his exemplary service attitude and his *gurudeva*'s blessings he was able to legally obtain the birthplace of Prabhupada Bhaktisiddhanta Saraswati Thakur, which is an extremely holy place for the entire Gaudiya Vaishnava community.

His Divine Grace Bhakti Pramod Puri Goswami Maharaj, who is now famously known as Bhakti Pramod Puri Goswami Thakur, in order to fulfill the will of his *gurudeva,* Prabhupada Bhaktisiddhanta Saraswati Thakur, spent his whole life in solitary places chanting the holy names and writing devotional articles for publication. Nowadays, those articles are being compiled into books such as *Art of Sadhana, The Heart of Krishna, The Heart of a Vaiṣṇava, Of Love and Separation,* and others. He was famously known in the Vaishnava community as the embodiment of the third *shloka* of Mahaprabhu's *Shikshashtakam: trinad api sunichena taror iva sahishnuna amanina manadena kirtaniya sada harih* – "One should be humbler than a blade of grass and more tolerant than a tree. One should offer respect to everyone and expect respect from no one. In this way, always chant the holy names of the Lord."

His Divine Grace Bhakti Rakshaka Sridhara Goswami Maharaj was a scholar in our spiritual lineage. He used to speak on the application of ancient scriptures to contemporary society. Many of his lectures have been compiled into books like *Śrī Guru and His Grace, The Golden Volcano of Divine Love, Loving Search for the Lost Servant,* and others. He also translated the *Bhagavad Gita* into Bengali. My spiritual master, His Divine Grace Srila Bhakti Pramod Puri Goswami Thakur, often said that His Divine Grace Bhakti Rakshaka Sridhara Goswami Maharaj was a replica of Srila Bhaktivinode Thakur in our *sampradaya*.

The acts of our previous teachers are called *radha-dasyam* because they followed in the footsteps of pure devotees. *Radha-dasyam* means to serve Krishna under the guidance of Radha and Her associates. Each of the books published by our *guru-varga* glorifies Srimati Radharani. Service to Radharani is equivalent to service to Krishna. Krishna becomes happy when we are able to please Radharani with our services.

Thus we can see that although some of our previous teachers sat in solitary places, they wanted to serve the loving mission of Lord Chaitanya and His associates, Sri Rupa and Raghunath. Therefore, those who chant independently with a sense of false prestige, lacking the mood of service to Hari, guru, and the Vaishnavas, will be unable to achieve the ultimate goal of spiritual practice.

Spiritual practice means to fix our mind and consciousness on serving the Lord under the shelter of the previous teachers. To help us learn to control our material senses, all our previous teachers taught us to serve pure devotees and chant the holy names. Prabhupada instructed us to serve by spreading the message of Rupa and Raghunath together. In this way we are engaged as eternal servants of Srimati Radharani. All our spiritual teachers are actually maidservants of Srimati Radharani. When we follow their instructions, we too are considered Her servants.

Text 17

'rādhā-nitya-jana', tāhā chāḍi mana,
kena vā nirjana-bhajana-kaitava
vrajavāsigaṇa, pracāraka-dhana,
pratiṣṭhā-bhikṣuka tā'rā nahe śava'
prāṇa āche tāṅra, se hetu pracāra,
pratiṣṭhāśā-hīna 'kṛṣṇagāthā' saba

Word-for-word

rādhā – Srimati Radharani; *nitya* – eternal; *jana* – associate; *tāhā* – that; *chāḍi* – giving up; *mana* – O mind; *kena vā* – why are you; *nirjana* – solitary; *bhajana* – spiritual practice; *kaitava* – hypocritical; *vrajavāsigaṇa* – residents of Vrindavan; *pracāraka* – exemplary preacher; *dhana* – treasure; *pratiṣṭhā-bhikṣuka* – beggar for material name, fame, and recognition; *tā'rā* – of that; *nahe* – are not; *śava'* – dead body; *prāṇa* – life force; *āche* – exists; *tāṅra* – their; *se hetu* – for that reason; *pracāra* – propagation; *pratiṣṭhāśā* – the hope of receiving material name, fame and recognition;

hīna – free from; *kṛṣṇagāthā* – arranged by Krishna; *saba* – everything.

Translation

O mind, why are you sitting in a solitary place, pretending that you are chanting but giving up the association of the eternal associates of Radharani? The previous teachers in our lineage, all of whom are residents of Vrindavan, are the treasure of Lord Chaitanya's preaching mission. Even while sitting in a solitary place in the holy *dhama* they are not begging for material name, fame, or recognition, which they consider to be like a dead body. Exemplary behavior and subsequent propagation of Krishna's glories, without any desire for material name, fame, recognition, or other expectations, is the life force of devotional practice.

Commentary

Prabhupada Bhaktisiddhanta Saraswati Thakur once said, "In order to fulfill the instructions of the previous teachers, who are pure devotees, one must be prepared to serve even if one has to become proud or slave like an animal or go to hell forever." We can see this mood in the residents of Vrindavan (Vrajavasis).

There is a story I would like to tell in this regard. Once, Narada Muni was thinking that he was the Lord's greatest devotee. But no one can equal the devotion of Srimati Radharani and Her associates in Vrindavan. To prove this point, the Supreme Lord manifested a pastime in which He had a severe headache.

Wanting to cure his Lord's headache, Narada asked, "How can I relieve Your headache?" Krishna replied, "I need dust from the feet of My devotees." Narada, although thinking himself a pure devotee, did not dare to give dust from his own feet to relieve the Lord's headache because he was afraid to suffer in hell. Instead, he went to many destinations around the universe to gather dust from the feet of the Lord's other devotees. But everyone refused his request, sharing Narada's fear.

Narada gave up and, depressed, returned to Krishna. As soon as he arrived, Krishna asked, "Did you find Me any dust?"

"No," Narada replied, although again, he could have given his own.

Then Krishna asked, "Did you approach the

residents of Vrindavan?" Narada said he had not. Krishna said, "Is it possible for you to go to Vrindavan and ask them for dust from their feet?" Narada Muni agreed.

As soon as Narada arrived in Vrindavan, the residents eagerly wanted news of their beloved Krishna. Still depressed, Narada Muni told them everything that had transpired and how he was unable to find a cure for Krishna's headache. Immediately, the *gopis* exclaimed, "Let us go to hell forever! Please take the dust from our feet and relieve our beloved Krishna's headache!"

This is our path – to follow in the footsteps of the Vraja *gopis*. Therefore, Prabhupada Bhaktisiddhanta instructs us as he does. Every act we do should be focused on pleasing our beloved Krishna, without concern for our own suffering. To illustrate this, I would like to tell of an incident that occurred between Chaitanya Mahaprabhu and Vasudeva Datta.

During Krishna's Vrindavan pastimes, Vasudeva Datta appeared as the singer Madhuvrata. When Krishna Chaitanya Mahaprabhu was freely spreading divine love by chanting the holy names, there were a few persons who lacked pious credits and therefore had no interest in chanting.

Vasudeva Datta astonished Chaitanya Mahaprabhu by saying, "O master, please let me suffer the consequences of all the bad karma committed by everyone. Let me go to hell for eternity so that they can be forever delivered for your satisfaction."

The main goal in propagating Lord Chaitanya's mission is to deliver the living entities without expecting anything in return. Even if some preachers are cheated by society, they should never retaliate. If an intelligent man is bitten by a dog, for example, he shouldn't try to bite the dog back. Lord Chaitanya appeared with the mood and complexion of Radharani. Therefore, whoever preaches Lord Chaitanya's mission by his or her own example is considered to be following in the footsteps of Radharani's eternal associates. As we explained before, our goal in practice is to attain Radharani's mercy. When we get Her mercy, we will become eligible for Krishna's mercy. O mind! Please give up your desire for material name, fame, and recognition as you sit in a solitary place and pretend to be a follower of Lord Chaitanya's mission.

None of Srimati Radharani's followers endeavor for material name, fame, or recognition.

To them, obtaining material name, fame, or recognition is a dead endeavor. The life force of Lord Chaitanya's preaching mission is to surrender absolutely to the previous teachers. The previous teachers in our line are all pure devotees and servants of Srimati Radharani's associates.

Srila Bhaktivinode Thakur writes:

śrī kṛṣṇa caitanya prabhu jīve dayā kari'
sva-pārṣada svīya dhāma saha avatari
atyanta durlabha prema karibāre dāna
śikhāye śaraṇāgati bhakatera prāṇa

"Out of immense compassion for the suffering souls in the material world, the Supreme Lord, Sri Krishna, appeared on earth as Chaitanya Mahaprabhu, accepting the mood and complexion of Srimati Radharani and appearing along with His personal associates and divine abode. In order to distribute the extremely rare treasure of divine love, He taught the suffering souls how to surrender. This surrendering process is the life and soul of all devotees."

Whoever wants to propagate Lord Chaitanya's loving mission must surrender fully to the previous teachers with absolutely no desire for material name, fame, or recognition. Our Bhaktivinode Thakur is Kamala Manjari in the spiritual world. He taught us that compassion for the living entities (*jiva-daya*) does not mean providing for their daily physical needs. We are not the body but the soul, so actual compassion means to give living entities knowledge of the soul and teach them to mitigate the causes of suffering.

Suffering is a consequence of previous bad activities. In order to destroy those consequences and experience the taste of divine love, Lord Chaitanya taught us, by His own example, how to surrender, because surrender is the life and soul of devotional practice. It is only by divine love that we can reach the eternal blissful abode of the Divine Couple, Sri Sri Radha and Krishna, and engage in Their eternal service. The main focus of Gaudiya Vaishnavas in their preaching is to help people attain this ultimate goal. Any success in this process is personally arranged by Sri Krishna's mercy through His pure devotees.

Text 18

śrīdayita dāsa, kīrtanete āśa,
kara uccaiḥsvare 'harināma-raba'
kīrtana-prabhāve, smaraṇa haibe,
se kāle bhajana-nirjana sambhava

Word-for-word

śrī – Radharani; *dayita* – beloved of; *dāsa* – servant; *kīrtanete* – in the congregational chanting of the holy names; *āśa* – desire; *kara* – perform; *uccaiḥsvare* – loudly; *harināma-raba* – the resounding chanting of the holy names; *kīrtana-prabhāve* – through the influence of the chanting of the holy names; *smaraṇa* – remembrance; *haibe* – will occur; *se kāle* – at that time; *bhajana-nirjana* – solitary service; *sambhava* – is possible.

Translation

O Varshabhanavi-dayita Das [Srila Prabhupada's initiated name], keeping your desire fixed on the congregational singing of the holy names, resoundingly chant the names of Lord Hari with a loud voice. By this chanting you will be able to remember the transcendental name, form, qualities, and pastimes of Lord Krishna as well as your eternal service to the Divine Couple. When you reach this stage, then you will be qualified to perform solitary devotional practice.

Commentary

The revival of the Gaudiya Vaishnava preaching mission was pioneered by His Divine Grace Srila Bhaktivinode Thakur and His Divine Grace Srila Bhaktisiddhanta Saraswati Thakur Prabhupada. When Srila Prabhupada Bhaktisiddhanta was born, Bhaktivinode Thakur named him Bimal Prasad. By Bhaktivinode Thakur's order Bimal Prasad accepted initiation from His Divine Grace Srila Gour Kishor Das Babaji Maharaj, who named him Varshabhanavi-dayita Das, "dearmost servant of the daughter of King Vrishabhanu." Gaudiya Vaishnavas are servants of the servants of the servants of Srimati Radharani. Srila Prabhupada Bhaktisiddhanta is Nayanamani Manjari in the spiritual abode, serving Srimati Radharani under the guidance of Lalita Sakhi, who is an intimate associate of Srimati Radharani.

In order to remove the material bondage of every living entity, Srila Prabhupada instructs us to resoundingly chant the Hare Krishna *maha-mantra*. This was performed by Krishna when He appeared as Lord Chaitanya, with the mood and complexion of Srimati Radharani. Lord Chaitanya is the special, compassionate form of the Supreme Lord who appeared 534 years ago and taught the process of congregationally chanting the holy names.

While chanting we should fix the mind, intelligence, and consciousness (*citta*) on serving the Divine Couple, Sri Sri Radha and Krishna, in Vrindavan. *Nirjana-bhajana* means to constantly chant the holy names while mentally serving Sri Sri Radha-Krishna in Vrindavan. If instead we chant with a desire for material name, fame, or recognition, or we maintain other material desires, our practice cannot be considered *nirjana-bhajana*.

If devotees feel unqualified to think about serving the Divine Couple in Vrindavan, they can think about the pure devotee guru and Vaishnavas and their instructions, pastimes, merciful natures, and other qualities. If we follow in the footsteps of the pure devotees and remember them while chanting, that is also considered *nirjana-bhajana*. According to the teachings of our previous teachers, our guru and the Vaishnavas are the servants of the servants of the servants of Srimati Radharani. Remembering our guru and the Vaishnavas gives pleasure to Srimati Radharani. We know from our scriptures that the Supreme Lord considers serving His pure devotees better than serving Him. His Divine Grace Srila Prabhupada Bhaktisiddhanta Saraswati Thakur once quoted from the *Padma Purana* in his discourses and then explained the verse:

ārādhanānāṁ sarveṣāṁ viṣṇorārādhanaṁ
paraṁ
tasmāt paratararaṁ devī tadīyānāṁ
samarcanam

"Of all the types of worship on earth, worship of Lord Vishnu is supreme. However, when compared to serving Lord Viṣṇu, serving His pure devotees is considered even higher. Serving Srimati Radharani, Nanda-Yashoda, Sridama-Sudama, or Raktaka-Patraka is superior to serving Sri Krishna directly.

Sanskrit Pronunciation

The short vowel ***a*** is pronounced like the ***u*** in b***u***t, the long ā like the ***a*** in f***a***r.

The short ***i*** is pronounced as in p***i***n, the long ***ī*** as in p***i***que, the short ***u*** as in p***u***ll, and the long ***ū*** as in r***u***le.

The vowel ***ṛ*** is pronounced like the ri in rim, the ***e*** like the ***ey*** in *th**ey***, the ***o*** like the ***o*** in g***o***, the ***ai*** like the ***ai*** in ***ai***sle, and the ***au*** like the ***ow*** in h***ow***.

The *anusvara* (***ṁ***) is pronounced like the ***n*** in the French word *bo**n**,* and the *visarga (**ḥ**)* is pronounced as a final ***h*** sound. At the end of a couplet, ***aḥ*** is pronounced ***aha***, and ***iḥ*** as ***ihi.***

The guttural consonants—***k***, ***kh***, ***g***, ***gh***, and ***ṅ***—are pronounced from the throat in much the same manner as in English. ***K*** is pronounced as in ***k***ite, ***kh*** as in Ec***kh***art, ***g*** as in ***g***ive, ***gh*** as in di***g-h***art, ***ṅ*** as in si***ng***.

The palatal consonants—***c, ch, j, jh,*** and ñ—are pronounced with the tongue touching the firm ridge behind the teeth. ***C*** is pronounced as in ***ch***air, ***ch*** as in staun***ch-h***eart, ***j*** as in ***j***oy, ***jh*** as in hedgehog, and ñ as in ca***ny***on.

The cerebral consonants—***ṭ, ṭh, ḍ, ḍh,*** and ***ṇ***—are pronounced with the tip of the tongue turned up and drawn back against the dome of the palate. ***Ṭ*** is pronounced as in tub, ***ṭh*** as in ligh***t-h***eart, ***ḍ*** as in ***d***ove, ***ḍh*** as in re***d-h***ot, and ***ṇ*** as in ***n***ut.

The dental consonants—***t, th, d, dh,*** and ***n***—are pronounced in the same manner as the cerebrals but with the forepart of the tongue against the teeth.

The labial consonants—***p, ph, b, bh,*** and ***m***—are pronounced with the lips. ***P*** is pronounced as in ***p***ine, ***ph*** as in u***ph***ill, ***b*** as in ***b***ird, ***bh*** as in ru***b-h***ard, and ***m*** as in ***m***other.

The semi-vowels—***y, r, l,*** and ***v***—are pronounced as in ***y***es, ***r***un, ***l***ight, and ***v***ine, while the sibilants—ś, ***ṣ,*** and ***s***—are pronounced as in the German ***s***prechen, ***sh***ine, and ***s***un. ***H*** is as in ***h***ome.

About the Author

His Holiness Śrīla Bhakti Bibudha Bodhāyan Gosvāmī Mahārāja is the current President Ācārya of Śrī Gopīnātha Gauḍīya Maṭha. He is the successor of the great saint Śrīla Bhakti Pramode Purī Gosvāmī Ṭhākura.

He was born Asim Kumar Sau on August 21, 1964, in Kanpur, West Bengal, India. Born into a Vaiṣṇava family, from his earliest years he practiced *bhakti* under the guidance of his maternal grandfather, Śrīmān Madana Mohana Prabhu who was a stalwart disciple of Śrīla Prabhupāda Bhaktisiddhānta Sarasvatī Ṭhākura. Although his paternal family all worshiped Śakti in the form of Kālī, Asim was heavily influenced by the devotion of his grandfather. In this way, he was inclined to the worship of Śrī Śrī Rādhā-Kṛṣṇa in the mood of Śrī Caitanya Mahāprabhu, following in the line of Śrīla Prabhupāda.

In 1978, while Asim was at the tender age of fourteen, Śrīmān Madana Mohana Prabhu took a contingent of over forty family members to Śrī

Dhāma Māyāpur to celebrate the appearance festival of Śrīmān Mahāprabhu. While visiting the Yoga-pīṭha, birthplace of Śrī Caitanya, on the Lord's appearance day, and seeing so many learned devotees and *sannyāsīs* and hearing their divine discourses, Asim vowed to dedicate his life to the path of devotion. He envisioned himself one day entering the *sannyāsa-āśrama*. Unsure how his family would react to such an idea, he kept it a secret.

By this time Asim had already met the illustrious devotee, Śrīla Bhakti Pramode Purī Gosvāmī Ṭhākura, and in his heart, had accepted him as his *dīkṣā-guru*. Shortly after his epiphany at the Yoga-pīṭha, Asim thought, "Let me quit worldly life and surrender unto the lotus feet of Śrī Guru." In this way, one day he stayed away from school with a desire to meet Śrīla B. P. Purī Gosvāmī Ṭhākura. On arriving there, the Ṭhākura was engaged in his daily worship. Asim waited and watched him in awe for several hours not wanting to disrupt his meditation. Once he had finished his worship, he gave Asim full attention.

When Asim revealed his mind, the Ṭhākura replied, "You are an intelligent boy. You should complete your education before making such an important life decision." Acknowledging the good sense of such guidance, Asim again resolved himself to follow the order of his guru and complete his education. He went on to complete a Bachelor of Commerce at Kolkata University.

All the while, his devotion never waned. In January 1986, he received *nāma* initiation from Śrīla B. P. Purī Gosvāmī Ṭhākura. He was given the name Acyutānanda Dāsa. In January 1990, during the auspicious festivities of the appearance festival of Śrī Caitanya Mahaprabhu, he received initiation into the *gāyatrī-mantra.*

Śrīla B. P. Purī Gosvāmī Ṭhākura was gradually attracting a considerable following. The devotees, headed by Acyutānanda's family, repeatedly requested him to open a temple so that they could have a place to gather. After many requests, he relented by strictly stipulating that such an establishment should only be for *bhajana*—deep spiritual practice.

In May 1990, Śrī Gopīnātha Gauḍīya Maṭha held its grand opening and the deities of Śrī Śrī Rādhā-Gopīnātha, Śrī Jagannātha-Baladeva-Subhadrā, and Lakṣmī-Narasiṁhadeva were installed. During the festivities, Acyutānanda and his father met with Śrīla B. P. Purī Gosvāmī

Ṭhākura. He said to Acyutānanda's father, "Baba Sunil Kṛṣṇa, may I ask you a question?" He replied, "Yes, Gurudeva." The Ṭhākura continued, "You have four sons. Would you have any objection if I kept Asim with me for my personal services?" His father replied, "It would bring us much happiness if Asim decided to stay and engage in such perfect *sevā* (service) for you." On the 28th of May 1990, Acyutānanda left home and became the personal servant of his guru.

Acyutānanda was primarily engaged in direct service to his guru, but he also engaged in managing the affairs of the *maṭha*. In 1993, at the insistence of his guru, he accepted the renounced order of *sann-yāsa* and received the name Tridaṇḍī Bhikṣu Bhakti Bibudha Bodhāyan. He then started traveling and preaching extensively, making his first sojourns to foreign lands.

On Gaura Pūrṇimā, in the year 1997, Śrīla Bhakti Pramode Purī Gosvāmī Ṭhākura announced that Śrīla Bhakti Bibudha Bodhāyan would become his successor. On October 22, 1999, Śrīla B. P. Purī Gosvāmī Ṭhākura left this world to reenter the spiritual realm. From this time onwards, Śrīla B. B. Bodhāyan Mahārāja has been guiding Śrī Gopīnātha Gauḍīya Maṭha as well as his disciples and followers through his perfect example and divine teachings. He travels the world tirelessly in order to spread Śrīmān Mahāprabhu's message of divine love for Śrī Śrī Rādhā-Kṛṣṇa.